FORWARD
THROUGH
the
YEARS

D1565116

ON THE COVER: "Eden" © 2016 Kathy Thaden
www.thadenmosaics.com

Scripture quotations are from the New Revised Standard Version of
the Bible, copyright © 1989 the National Council of the Churches of
Christ in the United States of America.

ISBN: 9780880284431

Printed in USA

Forward
Movement

FORWARD
THROUGH
the
YEARS

THE BEST OF *FORWARD DAY BY DAY*

Forward Movement
Cincinnati, Ohio

FOR TODAY

O God:

Give me strength to live another day;

Let me not turn coward before its difficulties
*   or prove recreant to its duties;*

Let me not lose faith in other people;

Keep me sweet and sound of heart,
*   in spite of ingratitude, treachery, or meanness;*

Preserve me from minding little stings or giving them;

Help me to keep my heart clean, and to live
*   so honestly and fearlessly that no outward*
*   failure can dishearten me or take away the*
*   joy of conscious integrity;*

Open wide the eyes of my soul that I may see
*   good in all things;*

Grant me this day some new vision of thy truth;

Inspire me with the spirit of joy and gladness;
*   and make me the cup of strength to suffering souls;*
*   in the name of the strong Deliverer,*
*   our only Lord and Savior, Jesus Christ.* Amen.

—PHILLIPS BROOKS

Preface

Forward Day by Day has encouraged, challenged, inspired, prodded, and empowered millions of people around the world since its conception in 1935. Born in a time when the United States and the Episcopal Church were facing deep divisions and serious challenges, *Forward Day by Day* immediately became a place where people sought daily connection with scripture and with God. More than eighty years later, *Forward Day by Day*, a cornerstone of the ministry of Forward Movement, continues with the same conviction that regular, consistent prayer is fundamental for disciples who seek strong spiritual lives.

Guided by this central tenet, *Forward Day by Day* has also undergone change. What began as a six-times-a-year print devotional is today published quarterly—in large and regular print, as an app and a podcast, on social media, and in English, Spanish, and Braille. Our writers have always relied on a mix of scripture, reflection, and prayer to craft the meditations, but the writers themselves have changed over the years. From a cadre of white, mostly older clergymen, our roster of authors has come to reflect the whole church: lay and ordained; women and men; young and old. Our writers are black and white, Latino, Asian, and Native American. They are straight, gay, married, single, widowed. Not every reader loves every writer, but every writer has something of value for every reader.

The community of *Forward Day by Day* has changed over the years as well. No longer is the conversation maintained solely at the kitchen table or in-person prayer groups. Today, *Forward Day by Day* has a half million readers, with print subscribers in more than fifty countries as well as online readers from around the world. A vibrant online community connects every day on Facebook, Twitter, and other social media outlets to wrestle with the reflections and scriptures—and to hold one another in prayer.

What hasn't changed about *Forward Day by Day* is the timeless wisdom offered in the meditations. As we compiled this collection of the best of *Forward Day by Day*, we were struck by the continuing relevance of entries. One meditation talks about a stranger who knocks on a church door. The man is an immigrant with halting English. The writer wonders how the congregation will respond and beseeches readers to live into the words from Hebrews: "Do not neglect to show hospitality to strangers, for by doing that some have entertained angels without knowing it." The year? 1948. A few years earlier, the church visitor had escaped the tyranny of Adolf Hitler. But hide the date, and you might think the author was writing today of our response to refugees fleeing Syria or Mexican immigrants coming to the United States in search of higher-paying jobs. In fact, we encourage you to read the meditations before looking at the dates listed at the end of each devotion. You might often be surprised by when the reflection was written. God's words—and deep reflection upon them—are timeless. And this compilation can be used year after year, which is why we've included a meditation for Leap Day and why we haven't specified dates for Ash Wednesday, Easter, or other holy days. We want this compilation to be a companion day by day and year by year.

While the wisdom of these meditations transcends calendars, many also reflect the times. The persistent worry of the Great Depression and the terror of World War II is present in meditations from the 1930s and 1940s. By the 1960s, angst and anger with the status quo become common themes. In the 1990s and early 2000s, abundance threads through the discourse. And in 2016, fear surfaces again, spurred by acts of local and global terrorism and all manner of economic and social inequalities.

Because we believe so strongly in the mission of *Forward Day by Day*, we have made it a vital part of our ministry at Forward Movement. Our staff gathers every weekday morning to read the daily devotion and then pray together, both for our local requests and for those sent in by readers and friends from around the world. In addition, we actively seek donor support to continue our ministry of giving nearly 30,000 copies of *Forward Day by Day* each quarter to members of the military, people in hospitals and nursing homes, and prison inmates. We receive letters and calls every day from these recipients who tell us how their lives have been changed by the words of God delivered in the pages of *Forward Day by Day*. In fact, one of our most beloved writers, whose work appears in this compilation, was a convicted murderer who, while incarcerated, found a constant companion in *Forward Day by Day*—and ultimately forgiveness and redemption through the ever-abiding, amazing grace of God.

May it be so for all of us.

—Editors, *Forward Day by Day*

A Morning Resolve

I will try this day to live a simple, sincere, and serene life, repelling promptly every thought of discontent, anxiety, discouragement, impurity, and self-seeking; cultivating cheerfulness, magnanimity, charity, and the habit of holy silence; exercising economy in expenditure, generosity in giving, carefulness in conversation, diligence in appointed service, fidelity to every trust, and a childlike faith in God.

In particular I will try to be faithful in those habits of prayer, work, study, physical exercise, eating, and sleep, which I believe the Holy Spirit has shown me to be right.

And as I cannot in my own strength do this, nor even with a hope of success attempt it, I look to thee, O Lord God my Father, in Jesus my Savior, and ask for the gift of the Holy Spirit.

January

THE DISCIPLES WAY

WORSHIP · SHARE · TURN · FOLLOW · LEARN · SERVE · PRAY

FORWARD
— day by day —

Bible readings and
Meditations for the
CHURCH YEAR

Late
Trinity
Oct. — Nov.

1935

JANUARY 1

Numbers 6:24-26. *The Lord bless you and keep you; the Lord make his face to shine upon you, and be gracious to you; the Lord lift up his countenance upon you, and give you peace.*

This is the blessing our Lord heard, the one commonly used in the synagogue then as today. Henry Sloane Coffin suggests that it relates to the stages of life. "The Lord bless and keep you" is a petition for youth. As we look on untarnished youth, we ask God to keep them from temptation, crushing sorrow, loss of ideals, fading vision, being victims of a system.

The Lord's brightness and graciousness may pertain to our middle years, which need to become years of grace. Life may become a fog, where getting on and making money confuse principle. We can come to see the second-choice situations in middle age as enlarged opportunities.

Age brings both failure and achievement. It gives perspective, when the drama is better understood than when we played in the foreground. May "that unhoped serene that men call age" of which poet Rupert Brooke wrote, and its sense of tranquility after the storm, bring you Christ's peace.—1941

JANUARY 2

Ephesians 1:16. *I do not cease to give thanks for you as I remember you in my prayers.*

We often devote all our time with God to asking for what we want. Rarely do we remember to thank him for what he has already given us. Yet it is an afflicted soul who cannot find something or someone to be thankful for, and an unusual soul who cannot find much to be thankful for. But we are so intensely conscious of what we lack and want that we overlook and take for granted what we have.

Few human relationships would long endure on such a basis. Even dear friends or parents might think it best to begin holding back their gifts until some signs of gratitude appear. But God is infinitely generous and never limits his favors to those who are properly thankful. It is not God who is injured by our ingratitude, but us.

We owe God innumerable gifts—all the way from the smallest favor to his "inestimable love in the redemption of the world by our Lord Jesus Christ" (The General Thanksgiving in *The Book of Common Prayer*). Yet our thanks to him are appallingly in arrears. Let no day go by in which you do not number your causes for gratitude and voice your thankfulness in prayer.—1954

JANUARY 3

Hebrews 11:13. *They confessed that they were strangers and foreigners on the earth.*

The following words are from *The Pilgrim's Progress*, spoken by Mr. Valiant-for-Truth as he crossed the river into the Celestial City: "Then said he, I am going to my Father's, and though with great difficulty I am got hither, yet now I do not repent me of all the Trouble I have been at to arrive where I am. My Sword I give to him that shall succeed me in my Pilgrimage, and my Courage and Skill, to him that can get it. My Marks and Scars I carry with me, to be a witness for me, that I have fought His Battles who now will be my Rewarder."

This is the story of life, and the famous eleventh chapter of Hebrews tells the same story. Even though life makes us feel like strangers and pilgrims on the earth, God is with us and, if we do his will, the end will be with God, too. Life is a pilgrimage, but there are shrines by the side of every road where we may worship him and gain his strength for the next stage of the journey. We are not strangers, come what may, for we are known to God and he loves us. Therefore "valiant be 'gainst all disaster," by God's grace.—1951

JANUARY 4

John 14:8. *Philip said to him, "Lord, show us the Father, and we will be satisfied."*

Philip's words are ours: let us see God directly. If only God would show himself to us on our terms, it would be easier to believe. During dark times we search particularly for some sign that God is with us, and that would satisfy us so that we would know deep down that there is nothing to fear.

Jesus' answer to Philip is direct and to the point: "Whoever has seen me has seen the Father." As in a detective story, the answer was there under their noses all the time. The Father has never stopped revealing himself. You just have to know where to look.

You can see God by looking to Jesus even today. Look for a single incident or gesture in which Jesus shines out from a person, something that lets you know God is at it again—daily revealing himself. When you see it, whisper "thank you" in your heart to God.
—1990

JANUARY 5

John 15:9. *As the Father has loved me, so I have loved you.*

Jesus, tell me, show me, how the Father loved you when he let you die an agonizing, cruel, brutal death and didn't do a thing to stop it. How does that express his love? And you love me with that kind of love?

U.S. Senator John McCain tells the story of how one of his guards in the Vietnamese prison camp came to his cell every evening, risking his own life to loosen McCain's bonds and make him a bit more comfortable for the night. Because of the language barrier, they couldn't communicate. But one night the guard drew the sign of the cross on the dirt floor. How many other acts of selfless love have been evoked over the centuries by this sign of the cross?

I think the Father didn't make you die on a cross, Jesus, or order you to die that way. I think he permitted you to show your love for us by your willingly enduring the worst we could do to you and then continuing to love us. Jesus, teach me to love that way. Transform me into what you would have me be. Grant me the courage, the power, and the fortitude to become worthy of being called a Christian.
—2003

JANUARY 6

Matthew 2:1-2. *In the time of King Herod, after Jesus was born in Bethlehem of Judea, wise men from the East came to Jerusalem, asking, "Where is the child who has been born King of the Jews?"*

The Epiphany—the "shining through"—of Christ was for all humanity. This fact is symbolically set forth in the visit of the Magi to his manger-cradle. These wise men of the East are thought to have been learned Persians from distant Iran, steeped in the lore of Zoroastrianism, the other great monotheistic religion of ancient times. It was appropriate that they should make that pilgrimage, for the followers of Zoroaster also had a tradition that in due time the One Only God would send to human beings a mediator who would lead them to himself.

In the Epiphany story we see the solidarity of humanity, the witness that God has maintained among all who seek him in sincerity and truth, and of his willingness to receive all, without distinction. Here also we have confirmation that in the works of nature there is an epiphany of God, for was it not a star that led the Magi? As the psalmist puts it, "The heavens declare the glory of God; and the firmament shows his handiwork."—1952

JANUARY 7

John 2:9. *The servants who had drawn the water knew.*

At the marriage feast in Cana of Galilee, it was Mary who saw the need and interceded, saying to Jesus, "They have no wine." And it was Jesus who changed the water into wine. But it was left to the servant to do the work. Mary said, "Do whatever he tells you." Jesus said, "Fill the jars with water," and then, "Now draw some out, and take it to the chief steward." And it was only when they did that— only in the act of pouring itself—that the water was seen to have become wine.

We are the servants: the church is a society of servants. We're to serve the guests at God's party—all the guests, whether we would have invited them ourselves or not. God gives the wine of his presence through us. He runs his household through us. He feeds his hungry guests through our hands. We fill the jugs with water and pour it out because that's the way God has arranged it.

He could do otherwise. God could get along without the church. But he doesn't choose to. He gives his guests into the hands of his household. The great outpouring of God's charity is in our hands. —1970

JANUARY 8

Psalm 118:24. *On this day the Lord has acted; we will rejoice and be glad in it.*

What a motivating, get-up-and-get-going statement this is. Any morning I can awaken with this verse in my heart and on my lips has a good chance of being great and productive. Any day I can wake up without picking up a load of past failures and fears, angers and sorrows, is a day I can live in the joy and power of my Christian faith. Yesterday is gone. This is the day!

On those mornings when I awaken with the sense of joyful possibilities, I know those possibilities are apt to reach fruition before nightfall. This is the day that the Lord has made and has acted, and I will rejoice and be glad in it, and I will use its hours in ways that please God and serve my brothers and sisters.

Yesterday and tomorrow are out of our reach and in God's hands. Let us thank God for today and make the most of it. Let us allow God's grace to make the most of us.—1991

JANUARY 9

Acts 10:40-42. *God raised him on the third day and allowed him to appear, not to all the people but to us who were chosen by God as witnesses...He commanded us to preach to the people and to testify that he is the one ordained by God as judge of the living and the dead.*

What is the church's main business? We must not give a long string of complicated answers to that question. Do not think of a building where people have the opportunity amidst seemly surroundings to worship God, to train their children, to enjoy fellowship, to serve as a Christian nucleus in a community. All that is good, but it does not come first.

A mighty wind blew on the church's first Day of Pentecost. There was a fierceness, an intensity when the church struck the first blow of its main business. It was to herald the good news. To teach the saving faith. To win followers of the one and only Lord. To go out and out until the last person is reached. If we want restored "the lost radiance of the Christian religion," we shall find it only in a rekindled passion to make Christ known to a waiting and a dying world. Missions! —1947

JANUARY 10

Mark 1:11. *And a voice came from heaven, "You are my Son, the Beloved; with you I am well pleased."*

The father stood before us on the chancel steps and announced a special guest, the preacher for the day. He listed his qualifications and professional accomplishments, and then he turned, and looked him full in the face and said, "You are my beloved son; with you I am well pleased." Those are the words we all want to hear.

A man in prison told me he knew his father loved him, he had to have loved him—but he never told him. Not once did his father ever speak those words. And I knew that this was why—because the father had never spoken those words—this man was now in prison, where he would remain until he heard them. These are the words of life.

Jesus is a grown man, but his life as we know it, the life by which we have been nurtured, only begins when these words have been spoken. With these words, Jesus undertakes what he was born to do, and not before. If you have never heard these words that announce life, then know this: you hear them now from God in Christ, for they are spoken for you, too—that your life may begin anew in the power and presence of the Risen One who came to live among us as one of us.—1997

JANUARY 11

Mark 1:14-15. *Jesus came to Galilee, proclaiming the good news of God, and saying, "The time is fulfilled, and the kingdom of God has come near."*

The gospel (good news) of God is that the kingdom of God is "near." It is here for everyone who will receive it, but what does Jesus mean, precisely, by the kingdom of God? It is easy to miss its divine depth and breadth by taking only part of Jesus' meaning and saying, "This is it!" As Coleridge said, "Make any truth too definite and you make it too small."

Essentially, the kingdom of God is the rule of God. Where God's will, rather than ours, is done, there is the kingdom. And the glory of the kingdom is that wherever it is found there we find health, wholeness of life, joy, and peace. Why must we still pray, "Thy kingdom come?" Because, as Aldous Huxley puts it, too few of us have learned to pray, "My kingdom go."

Our self-will, our determination to have things our way rather than God's way, is the only reason why God's kingdom is not the only kingdom we see and experience on earth. But the good news is that the kingdom is near. It is in fact right here. If we want it.—1965

JANUARY 12

Mark 1:33. *And the whole city was gathered around the door.*

I see people every morning waiting for the bus. Every morning the bus comes and the people get on. No matter how often it happens, they are acting out a miracle. "Well, now," you say, "after all, it was a bus stop. If they had been waiting on the top floor of a building and a bus had come by, well, that might be a miracle!" No, you're missing the point. The miracle was not the bus. It was the waiting.

Waiting requires faith, and even a little faith is a miracle. To believe in the past or present is not hard, but to have hope for what is not yet—this only comes by living in the light of a world to come. On that evening "the whole city was gathered around the door"— waiting. Like us, they had the usual needs of every person in every generation, hoping for some kind of help, some manner of salvation. Then as they waited in patience and in pain, they heard, perhaps, the sound of a footstep just inside the door, and Jesus appeared. And looking at Jesus they knew their waiting was over. Before they experienced the miracle of healing, they had to demonstrate the miracle of hope.—1962

Mark 2:3-5. *Then some people came, bringing to him a paralyzed man, carried by four of them. And when they could not bring him to Jesus because of the crowd, they removed the roof above him; and after having dug through it, they let down the mat on which the paralytic lay. When Jesus saw their faith, he said to the paralytic, "Son, your sins are forgiven."*

Back in Capernaum, Jesus preaches to Peter's crowded street, perhaps from the stair landing outside his room. Four men, unable to get near, hoist their palsied friend to the flat housetop and lower him down behind Jesus through the trap door. We know from the gospels how Jesus loved this almost violent determination in people when they wanted to help. He doesn't want people to sit and twiddle their fingers and say, "It can't be done." Jesus will heal and pardon the most helpless of sinners. Have I three friends who with me would bring one to him? Do you know someone who is sick or in great trouble? Join with a few friends and carry him to God in strong, expectant prayer. Expect great things of God.—1936

JANUARY 14

Isaiah 42:10. *Sing to the Lord a new song.*

The long night of the exile was almost over, for God was about to do a great "new thing" for his people. The prophet called for a new song, a song of praise to the Lord in which the whole world was invited to join. It would be strange if, in face of the marvelous love and care of God which they had personally experienced, the people of God did not sing their songs of praise. It would be strange—and yet, can it be denied that some Christians seem to belie the joy of their faith?

In a little book about some remarkable early-day Salvationists, Edward H. Joy wrote about old Harry. A disreputable but happy character, Harry met the Salvation Army, was converted, and became known for his infectious, happy religion. As he made public his commitment to Christ, he laughed and there was no irreverence, though some who saw him were scandalized.

After years of joyous service for Christ, Harry lay dying, a smile still on his face. Just before he died, he said, "Who'd have thought it, old Harry getting into heaven! It's enough to make me laugh!" The Christian faith will appear more attractive when some of us are freed from our inhibitions to reveal more of the joy of the Lord.—1975

JANUARY 15

Psalm 116:15. *I will offer you the sacrifice of thanksgiving and call upon the Name of the* Lord.

"It is not the happy people who are thankful. It is the thankful people who are happy," Bishop Frere wrote in *Sursum Corda*. "Count your blessings one by one" is not Pollyanna stuff. It works. "Think" and "thank" are related in the Christian experience. For example, think about God enough and you will thank him for what he is, for what he has done, for the much more he would do if we would cooperate with him. "Think" comes from the same root, too.

If you think about God and thank him, things will change. It is according to spiritual law. Thanksgiving is faith in action. And faith attracts God's gifts, attracts God.

The Bible speaks of going into God's gates with thanksgiving. It says God meets the person who rejoices; God inhabits praise. It tells stories of battles won and prisons opened when praise prepared the way for God. If prayer changes things, so does thanksgiving.—1943

JANUARY 16

John 1:40-41. *One of the two who heard John speak and followed him was Andrew, Simon Peter's brother. He first found his brother Simon and said to him, "We have found the Messiah."*

Look at this! Andrew, the first man to receive Christ, was ordinary, what we call "the common or garden variety." He had no genius or fine theories. He was not a great leader but he was a prince of a follower. His plain common sense detected Jesus' greatness at once.

Andrew asked no questions. The matter was settled for him: follow. At once he goes to work and brings his gifted brother. Wherever we read of Andrew, he is introducing someone to Jesus.

Reader, do you rate yourself as plain, ordinary, everyday? Remember what Lincoln said: "God must love the common people; he made so many of them." God does. And so does his church. We have leaders aplenty. Christ calls for followers, workers, plain men and women who accept what good and truth they see and act upon it. Leave brilliance to someone else. Hold to your simple faith. Take your place. Witness where you are. Be a plain disciple, steadily drawing others to Christ.—1936

JANUARY 17

Ephesians 4:6. *One God and Father of all, who is above all and through all and in all.*

A famous philosopher based his argument for God and religion on "the starry heavens above and the moral law within." Many great astronomers have been devout believers in God. God's apparent ordering of the stars in their courses has also made it natural to believe in laws for the guidance of his children on the way of life.

The Ten Commandments are not a worn-out moral code, but plumb the very depths of life in every individual and in every generation. But there is a difference between the laws governing the stars in their courses and the laws ordained to guide us in our relationships of life.

The laws ordained to guide us await our understanding and cooperation. Because we are God's children, he cannot fulfill his purpose for us except as we join our will to his. We must be willing partners with God on the pilgrimage of life.—1937

JANUARY 18

Matthew 16:15. *He said to them, "But who do you say that I am?"*

This gospel reminds me of one of those moments on a long journey when you pause and look at how far you have come, then look ahead to the road still before you. Stopping midway, you reassess. Jesus' journey through the countryside has led to much talk. So Jesus asks his followers to sum up the trip so far: who do people say that he is? The familiar answers come: John the Baptist come back to life; Elijah, returned among us; some other prophet.

The question may have been directed at goodhearted, impetuous Peter, but Jesus is also asking me. Who do I say that he is? Into what parts of my heart will I invite him? What of me will I try to hide, pretend to be other than I am? How will I follow him? At a safe distance, watching to see how it will turn out? Or will I take up my cross, as he invites me, and follow him? Will I hold back, or plunge deliriously into deep waters? Is my baptism a polite social ritual, an excuse to get the family together, or is it new birth? Who is this Christ for me, who has marked me as his own forever?—1999

JANUARY 19

Ephesians 5:2. *Live in love, as Christ loved us and gave himself up for us, a fragrant offering and sacrifice to God.*

When people meet you, God longs for them also to meet Christ. It sounds like a very high expectation, and quite beyond us, beyond even our best imaginings on our best days. Nevertheless, it is what God longs to see happen. God longs for us to live so that in us others will recognize and be touched by the love of Christ. When the writer of the letter to the Ephesians tells his readers to "live in love," he is really talking about that divine hope. To live in love is to be an advertisement for God. To act with decisive selflessness, even in a small way, is to reflect nothing less than the brilliant reality of the God who meets us in Christ.

Every step you take in love represents the purposes of God. It may be a small step—a minor kindness, a tiny sacrifice, a spontaneous act of mercy—but every step walked in love is evidence of the presence of God in the world. Moreover, it is a step along the road toward your truest self, the self made in the image of Christ, the self God made and means for you to be.—1996

JANUARY 20

Mark 4:21. *Is a lamp brought in to be put under the bushel basket, or under the bed, and not on the lampstand?*

An old friend of mine struggled with the question of whether he was called to ordained ministry. His belief in God was profound, and he believed God expected much from him. What he did not know was how to fulfill this expectation. Did it mean ordination? The life of a priest frightened him. He was attending church one day when this very lesson was read. When he heard the description of a lamp that was hidden, the lesson spoke directly to him. He believed he was guilty of hiding what God had given him, that he was not using the gifts he had been given as they were intended to be used. At that point he accepted the call to the priesthood.

We are all different and are called to different kinds of service. But each of us has been given gifts from God to use as God knows best. Some are called to be priests, others teachers, mothers, fathers, lawyers, politicians, craftspeople. Each of us must choose what to do with the lamp God has given. What we must not do is keep it to ourselves, hide it. The lamp belongs on a lampstand to illumine our world.—2000

JANUARY 21

Psalm 31:21. *Blessed be the* LORD*! for he has shown me the wonders of his love in a besieged city.*

It is hard to imagine a worse circumstance than siege. Besieged people live in their own familiar environment, watching it disintegrate, watching their neighbors die on their own doorsteps. Ancient Israel knew about besieged cities, as one great power after another swept across its borders. Out of that experience much of the poetry of Israel's faith is painfully wrought. What is also wrought is the resiliency of Israel's faith, as when the psalmist cried out, "Blessed be the Lord! for he has shown me the wonders of his love in a besieged city."

Amid the terror and loss, the destruction of all that was precious, the psalmist kept an eye out for evidence of the love of God. The psalmist was rewarded, touched by wonder, and upheld. There are times when each of us feels under siege, bombarded by forces which seem to destroy our very tranquility. In such times we must keep an eye out for signs of the love of God. For those signs are never more present than when the darkness is deepest, the sorrow most agonizing, the terror most real. God comes to us in such times to touch us with his love. "Blessed be the Lord!"—1995

JANUARY 22

Ephesians 6:11. *Put on the whole armor of God, so that you may be able to stand against the wiles of the devil.*

Unless you have seen it, you would not believe the pads and tape that a football player binds himself in before going forth to the gridiron wars. In order to stand before the onslaught of the enemy, he covers everything from head to foot. He protects himself well. Saint Paul advises Christians to do the same as they sally forth to fight the daily wars of life. It works.

Every morning, close your eyes and think of the invisible armor you may don to protect yourself this day. A band of truth about your middle, righteousness across your chest, peace wherever your feet go, an aura of faith encircling you, knowledge of God's saving grace protecting your head, carrying as your weapon the Spirit of Christ which is the Word of God. Of course your weapon is love for Christ who has taught us that this is the only way we can conquer eternally. Make this a part of your morning meditation and see what a difference it makes in your life.—1971

JANUARY 23

1 Corinthians 1:10. *I appeal to you, brothers and sisters, by the name of our Lord Jesus Christ, that all of you be in agreement and that there be no divisions among you, but that you be united in the same mind and the same purpose.*

What produces divisions among us? It would be foolish to pretend that we are any different from the people of Corinth to whom Saint Paul wrote. We have contentions, disagreements, arguments, grudges with our friends, our fellow-workers, our employers, even with our fellow church members. This is not to say that there isn't room for honest disagreement and discussion within the framework of love and personal respect, which are the proper foundation of church, family, neighborhood, job. But so often differing points of view become the basis for contentions, for bitterness, for claims of being absolutely right.

We act as if the questions with which we grapple have simple answers which demand absolute allegiance. "If I am right—and I am right—then you are wrong." On the contrary, Jesus Christ is our only absolute allegiance. Contentions between church groups, as between others, are usually rooted in mistaking partial allegiances for absolute allegiances. And so it is that even in the Body of Christ, the sin of division exerts its power over us.—1969

JANUARY 24

Mark 5:26. *She had endured much under many physicians.*

I overcommit myself. I struggle to keep my office running on time. The waiting room fills, parents become cranky, children grow restless. One day, already far behind schedule, I brought a family in for a first visit. The signs were ominous: they brought voluminous records, having seen my kind before and "endured much under many physicians."

I read the records they had brought, looked at the x-rays and the child, and tried not to show the sinking feeling I had. Another desperate family searching for something I could not provide. My predecessors' conclusions were undoubtedly correct. I had nothing to add. To tell them this today would take time I didn't have. "God, help me"—my commonest workday prayer.

"How can I help you?" I asked. "Give us a different diagnosis." "I can't do that," I said. "Then listen to our story." Suddenly it was clear. Doctors had examined their child, run many tests, said much to them—but no one had listened. I stopped and I listened. Nothing changed for them that day: not their child, not the diagnosis, not their future. Yet it was a marvel, because for a moment we had beaten back the darkness that engulfed them by being present for one another.—1999

JANUARY 25

Matthew 10:19-20. *Do not worry about how you are to speak or what you are to say; for what you are to say will be given to you at that time; for it is not you who speak, but the Spirit of your Father speaking through you.*

A friend found a table blessing that he wanted to use when guests came to dinner, but he wasn't sure he could remember it. His wife typed it out and placed it under the glass plate.

We think of putting on the "whole armor of God" as we face each day but perhaps having the Holy Spirit with us is also having a glass plate to read through. You begin each day believing that you know most of the answers and you will get through it safely. But what a great comfort to know that when you are stuck, all you must do is drop your head in prayer. The Holy Sprit will tell you, not in typewritten lines slightly magnified by the glass plate, but with a voice and in words of scripture, what to say and do.

God provides us with his guidance. May we never hesitate or be embarrassed to squint a little just to make sure we have the right words.—1973

JANUARY 26

Isaiah 49:9. *…saying to the prisoners, "Come out," to those who are in darkness, "Show yourselves."*

Over the past thirty years, much has been written about church growth and the drop in mainline church membership. I read what pertains to the Episcopal Church, and what I read is usually accompanied by complaints about the direction being taken and some aspect of inclusivity.

When we in the church feel weak or threatened, we tend to be a selective bunch. It has been many years since a then-new presiding bishop, Edmond Lee Browning, issued a historic pronouncement from the pulpit of Washington National Cathedral: "There shall be no outcasts in this church." Yet, in many parishes it is a struggle to cast our loving, accepting eyes on all those around us.

At every vestry retreat I have ever attended on the subject of church growth, we have been warned that growth brings change and that change can be scary. Unfortunately, many of us have taken that warning to heart and have opted for comfort rather than change. It is time to reflect on today's verse from Isaiah and our call to proclaim, "Come out…Show yourselves."—1998

JANUARY 27

Mark 6:41. *Taking the five loaves and the two fish, [Jesus] looked up to heaven, and blessed and broke the loaves, and gave them to his disciples to set before the people.*

At a dinner for teachers, two of us clergymen sat together with our teacher-wives, wondering which of us would be called on for the invocation or to "give thanks" or "say grace" at the bidding of the master of ceremonies. To our surprise he called on a staff member of the county education department. This gentleman confidently prayed for the particular needs of teachers, thanking God for all his blessings and for our fellowship and food. It was a beautiful thing.

Several people looked at us to see if we were miffed at being passed over for a layman. No way. Would that every Christian would go and do likewise! This man reflected a background of family prayer, church attendance, and the guidance of a capable pastor.

I was once asked to attend a city council meeting for the purpose of opening it with a prayer. I suggested to the mayor that the council members open their meeting by praying with and for one another. The job of the clergy is sometimes to do, but more often to help others to do. Start learning today.—1973

JANUARY 28

Mark 6:50. *They all saw him and were terrified. But immediately [Jesus] spoke to them and said, "Take heart, it is I; do not be afraid."*

These men were terrified because they were in a storm at sea. Jesus would allay their fear—this time—by delivering them from that peril. If God always, unfailingly, delivered us from things that frighten us, we too would find it easy to live without fear and without reproach. But to some or all of these men in the boat Jesus would have to say, later on, that they must be hauled off to prison and to death for his name's sake. That would be a terrifying ordeal from which he would not deliver them as he did in the present trial. But concerning those coming trials he spoke as he speaks now: Do not be afraid! I am with you always! Christ does not promise that he will always deliver us from pain, trouble, or death. Sometimes God in his goodness can spare us such suffering, sometimes evidently not. What Christ promises is that if we put our hand in his and walk with him, he will always cast out our fear. On that we can count. Faith delivers us not from disaster but from the only ultimate disaster—despair.—1970

JANUARY 29

Psalm 119:97. *Oh, how I love your law! All the day long it is in my mind.*

In our friary, we read parts of Psalm 119 every day at midday prayer, covering the entire 176 verses each week. It's a remarkable psalm. It has been called a love song—not one of youthful passion, but of sustained reflection on God's law, which has become for the psalmist as familiar as a lifelong partner. The psalmist delights in naming God's "law," "precepts," "commandments," "decrees," "statutes," "way," "promise," "word," "ordinances," and so on in a kaleidoscope of variations on a theme.

It's also a very personal psalm. Nearly every verse has personal pronouns such as "I," "my," or "your." God is not an abstract being, only approachable indirectly. God can be addressed and known personally.

This "law of God" is not the legalism condemned by Jesus, but an encounter with the living God. "Law" (Torah) is not an endless series of regulations to be obeyed but an invitation to follow God on the way. It is a way of life, the way of love.—2010

There is no fulfillment of the law apart from communion with God, and no communion with God apart from fulfillment of the law. —Dietrich Bonhoeffer

JANUARY 30

Matthew 5:8. *Blessed are the pure in heart, for they will see God.*

A friend and his family recently visited a large church on the East Coast. His five-year-old son asked if he could light a candle. A sign read "Suggested donation: $1.00 per candle." The man calculated: "Three kids times x candles—too much on a tight budget." So he said no. He had paid for a tour, and that was enough.

Later they visited the Washington National Cathedral. While marveling at its beauty and stature, the father, from two hundred feet away and down a side aisle, saw his son lighting every candle in the votive bank. In horror, he hurried toward his son. A priest then stepped to his son, lifted him up, and let him light every candle on the top row. As the priest put the child down, the boy said, "Look, Dad, I honored God with all the candles!"

Ashen-faced, the father reached for his wallet and said, "I am so sorry, Father. What do I owe?" "Not a cent," the priest replied. "The joy in his face as he lit each candle, thanking God for someone or something in his life—that was the great offering today. Please come back and visit us again." The purity of a child's heart and a kindly priest led my friend back to church.—2005

JANUARY 31

Psalm 57:7. *My heart is firmly fixed, O God, my heart is fixed; I will sing and make melody.*

There is a faculty called attention, which we ought to use more than we do. It is the fixing of our minds on some one thing. What you look at, what you are interested in, what you pay attention to, is what molds your character. Every teacher knows this. But this fact is even more important for the spiritual life than for education.

The trouble with some of us is that we haven't been paying attention to the things of the soul, not giving much thought to God. We have been putting our minds on other things. We have neglected the things that would have reminded us of God—worship in church, reading the Bible, the life of prayer and service.

If we choose, we can attend to God. This would seem to have been Christ's great object—to fix our attention on him, to make us grow intensely interested in him. Conversion takes place only when someone takes an entire and intense interest in Jesus Christ, and the Christian life consists in paying constant attention to him.—1941

February

FEBRUARY 1

John 6:35. *Jesus said to them, "I am the bread of life."*

A realtor once said that the best way to sell a house is to bake bread, because the aroma will evoke a powerful sense of "home" in potential buyers. This association of home and bread runs deep in our psyches. Recall, for example, the Israelites' years of desert wandering in search of their promised homeland. They were nourished by bread from heaven.

In John's account, Jesus echoes this nurturing image: "I am the bread of life...I am the bread that came down from heaven." He reminds us that as Christians we, too, live by bread from heaven, nurtured and nourished by God. No longer is it manna that feeds us, but Christ himself who is present in the eucharist.

So the next time you stretch out your hands to receive communion, remember that God's hand is already stretched out to you, welcoming you home. And the next time you smell baking bread, think of it as aromatic incense, a humble reminder of God's tender, constant presence among us.—2003

FEBRUARY 2

Luke 2:25, 36. *Now there was a man in Jerusalem whose name was Simeon...There was also a prophet, Anna, the daughter of Phanuel, of the tribe of Asher.*

I find Simeon and Anna an infinitely moving pair. In Anna's case, the vocation to love and worship God has replaced all else in her life. One can imagine her: shabby, old, poor, and, in the eyes of relatives and acquaintances, probably rather dotty. Simeon, also old and devout, is longing, as the prophets taught him to do, for the Messianic age to come.

These two are a kind of miracle because, unlike many of us who are rigid with expectation, they know how to recognize their joy when it comes. They might have been so preoccupied with their own piety that they were no longer open to God's revolutionary truth. The one lesson each had learned was how to wait, so that when God filled their emptiness they knew what to make of it.

The long years of waiting must have been painful ones. Human beings are so much bound up in time that we tend to want our joys now, and to grieve inwardly when we don't get them. Simeon and Anna must have drunk from the cup of frustration and doubt. And now, in the joyous encounter with the child Jesus, their hope and obedience have been fulfilled.—1976

FEBRUARY 3

Psalm 72:6. *He shall come down like rain upon the mown field, like showers that water the earth.*

There are few more striking things said about God in the Bible—or anywhere else—than these words. God comes down like thunder, like lightning, in a thousand other manifestations of his power. Of course—but who except our psalmist compares him to the rain, the showers that water the earth? Shakespeare's Portia comes close when she says of mercy that it drops "as the gentle rain from heaven upon the place beneath." But she's talking about an attribute of God. The psalmist is talking about God himself, coming down like that gentle, nourishing, life-giving rain.

God is coming down like rain in your own life. You may not be vividly aware of it at this moment, or at any moment, because it is so gentle and quiet—that coming down. Yet it is this very shower of God himself that keeps you alive, as the rain keeps the grass of the field alive. How could you live without it? As Augustine wrote: God is *semper agens, semper quietus*—"always active, always quiet." —1983

FEBRUARY 4

Genesis 23:4. *I am a stranger and an alien residing among you.*

As I walked down the cathedral's huge center aisle, I saw large black and white photographs on the wall—pictures of frightened men and women with yellow stars on their clothing; children with wild, questioning eyes; cattle cars crammed with people. As I approached the chancel I saw a statue of a human being dying in agony—his arms stretched to heaven as if to make one last plea for confirmation that mercy and goodness existed somewhere in the world.

The occasion was a service for Yom HaShoah, commemorating the Jews murdered before and during World War II. I ached to think that centuries of Christian animosity had played a role in "the Final Solution." The church had played a part by negating all things Jewish—its spirituality, experience, identity, and validity.

Pierre Teilhard de Chardin wrote that "faith has need of the whole truth." As we seek to grow in our understanding of our tradition, we must also learn the darker side of the church's history, so that we do not carry those mistakes into our present or our future.—1990

FEBRUARY 5

Psalm 69:10. *Zeal for your house has eaten me up.*

There is an insistent quality about God and his demands which we often forget, often allow to be hidden from us by other things. The biblical word for this is "jealous." God is a jealous God. Of course, he is not jealous in the "green-eyed monster" sense, but he is jealous in the sense he will not be satisfied with the normal subpar allegiance, the half-hearted commitment. God is not satisfied because such a halfhearted commitment will only bring us grief and misery and, ultimately, death.

God loves us, and knows that our true good, happiness, and even genuine human life itself, depend on our relationship with him. Of course he must be jealous for us (not of us). The Good News is that Christ's bitter death, in some way we do not understand, is the help that leads us to and lets us make that full and growing commitment. The zeal for God's house ate Jesus up, and he knew it would, for he was jealous for the people of God with God's own kind of jealousy. Through his zeal, grace. Through his grace, our commitment to life. —1964

FEBRUARY 6

Hebrews 12:12. *Lift your drooping hands and strengthen your weak knees.*

When pioneers in covered wagons crossed the prairies and mountains to go west, there was no room for extra baggage. They had to sit loose and travel light.

This was the situation for the Hebrews in the wilderness. Nomads on the march, they could not afford a clutter of possessions. They traveled with the bare necessities. Something of this same trimness entered into their religious life as well. There was a simplicity about the Mosaic religion: the laws could be counted on your fingers; ritual was at a minimum.

Lent will be here before long. As we prepare for it, we might learn the discipline of traveling light. It applies to our theological dogmas as well as our material comforts. Paul reminds us in his Letter to the Hebrews to lay aside every weight as we run the course ahead. Some of the burden consists of our sins, of course. We are all hindered by our selfishness, our lack of concern for others. A good deal of the weight, however, is just ecclesiastical baggage—the outworn good we carry long after its utility has disappeared.

The world is on the march. If we are to minister, we had best strip for action and learn to travel light, lifting our drooping hands and strengthening our weak knees, following our Lord's example. —1971

FEBRUARY 7

Luke 5:8. *Go away from me, Lord, for I am a sinful man!*

When Isaiah had his vision of God, he felt an immediate sense of his own uncleanness. Peter, in the presence of Christ, became aware of his sinfulness. One of the effects of the holiness of God is to cause us to see our sin and our own unworthiness in stark reality. In the contrast we see what we might be, and what we truly are.

In that instant when Peter asks Jesus to depart from him because he is sinful, Jesus does not leave him. Peter may have been surprised and shocked by the self-realization of his sin, but God was not. God knew it all the time. It often requires a shock, a contrast, to enable God to break through our self-satisfaction and our pride. When we feel ashamed and unworthy, our defenses are down. So the Lord doesn't depart from us. The depth of our sin may surprise us. All through our blindness Christ is beside us, and when we begin to see ourselves as we really are, he is able to bestow on us his forgiveness and renewing strength. He has been with us all the time.

Awareness of our sin is the awareness of our need for God. Let us welcome it.—1981

FEBRUARY 8

Hebrews 13:1-2. *Let mutual love continue. Do not neglect to show hospitality to strangers, for by doing that some have entertained angels without knowing it.*

God has interrupted me. Not with a lightning bolt, but just with a quiet visitor.

There I was, working on a writing project about displaced persons, when an actual displaced person showed up at my door. Hitler drove this man from his native country years ago. Now he is a good American and serves America well. Now he is married and there's a baby coming. And he's looking for a church. "Which church?" he asks. "You have so many different ones!"

I talked to him about our church and gave him some things to read. But something troubles me. There are two churches within walking distance of his home (he has no car, and remember the baby), but to which shall I send him? With his faulty English and still foreign manner, am I right to invite him to our church, or should I send him to the other one? Would either of them make him welcome? Would either be a home in Christ for this man and his family? They need the real thing—a fellowship of practicing Christians who will show forth grace, understanding, the love of Christ. Will either church do the real thing or only a surface job?

Would your parish receive this couple as our Lord would? I pray so.—1948

FEBRUARY 9

John 8:6. *Jesus bent down and wrote with his finger on the ground.*

What did you write, Lord, when that woman and her accusers stood before you? What words did your finger trace in the sand? Did any of the crowd read it—or had they all gone? Did the woman—anxious, fearing for her life—read the message on the ground? Or was she too relieved, too grateful, too full of your forgiving grace to look down at your words?

The wind has blown away whatever you wrote that day. A million feet have obliterated your words. Yet your action haunts me.

There she stood—terrified, humiliated—wondering how it would feel when the first rock struck her, looking in the face of death and shame. And you wrote on the ground.

Whatever words your fingers traced, I am sure it was a love note to all of us as we stand guilty before God's judgment. It was a pardon for our sins. It was a message of forgiveness and acceptance.—1984

FEBRUARY 10

Genesis 27:12. *Perhaps my father will feel me, and I shall seem to be mocking him, and bring a curse on myself and not a blessing.*

The story of Jacob stealing Esau's blessing is one of the hardest in all scripture to understand from a moral standpoint. Like the banishment of Hagar and Ishmael, it presents a morally reprehensible act as a vehicle of God's purposes. Jacob will have to flee to escape his brother's wrath, but there is little question that it is God's will being acted out here. The people of God see themselves, after all, as Jacob's and not Esau's descendants.

Issues of personal guilt and selfish motives do not seem to apply. Whatever happened to fairness? Does the end justify the means?

We must remember that we are dealing here not with "pleasant old tales" but with real people like us. How many of us have benefited by taking advantage of others, unfairly? We need not be moral monsters to have done so, just sinful human beings.

Our fear is that we will have to be responsible for those black marks on our record. Our hope, on the other hand, is that God still does seem able to use "tainted" lives for his purposes and to overrule the cruelty and deceit to which sin so often leads.—1980

FEBRUARY 11

Psalm 146:1. *Hallelujah! Praise the Lord, O my soul! I will praise the Lord as long as I live; I will sing praises to my God while I have my being.*

There is a certain great altarpiece by El Greco that I love. I go to the art institute no longer to gaze at it, but rather to see what it does to people. They come in bored or tired or simply casual. They look, and sometimes they are transformed. It is a glorious thing to see a human face transformed—even for a moment. Self is forgotten. Petulance, worry, vanity, pettiness—all wiped away, and instead, wonder and awe—something akin to worship.

Worship is the "direct, vital, joyous personal experience and practice of the presence of God," says Rufus Jones in *The Inner Life*. No one who truly worships can remain ugly or dull or hopeless, for in that worshiping face is reflected the glory of God. You can worship alone. The beginnings of worship are best found in aloneness. But when you bring to church your discoveries of God's goodness and add them to the praises and adoration of the whole congregation, then worship rises to its height. We are like an orchestra making great music to the perfect goodness of God. Come with us and worship.—1941

❧❧❧❧

FEBRUARY 12

Psalm 91:5-6. *You shall not be afraid of any terror by night, nor of the arrow that flies by day; of the plague that stalks in the darkness, nor of the sickness that lays waste at mid-day.*

Christian preachers down through the ages have frequently treated "the sickness that lays waste at mid-day" as the characteristic sickness of middle age, which strikes us in the noonday of life. This sickness is a compound of several things: boredom, disillusionment, weariness, the failure of the dreams of our youth to come true. Most middle-aged folk know this sickness well. God knows it too, and bids us in our misery to return to him.

As I look back over my ministry of a quarter-century, I recall very many victims of the noonday sickness whom I have presented for confirmation. The Holy Spirit had moved them to come to God in his church to find renewal of life.

Does the noonday sickness grip you? Remember now your Creator in the days of your middle age: offer your tired life to him, renew your allegiance to Jesus Christ. He can do many wonderful things with you and for you, which he could not do for you in your callow youth.—1963

FEBRUARY 13

Romans 14:10. *Why do you pass judgment on your brother or sister? Or you, why do you despise your brother or sister? For we will all stand before the judgment seat of God.*

The unwritten sequential sentence to the above might well be, "And then, where will you be?" Saint Paul was discussing differing customs among Christians. Some ate all kinds of food; some ate only vegetables. Some made one day of the week especially holy; others considered all days equally holy.

We can easily transfer the same thinking to various practices among Christians today: standing or kneeling or bowing the head; lots of candles or none; incense, sanctus bells, or the Quaker meeting. The 1928 Prayer Book or the 1979 Prayer Book; the Revised Standard Version of the Bible or any other version. You get the idea.

The test for Paul was whether in the observance of any of these customs, one thanked God. Thanking God is central; how one does it is relative. He who judges by the custom and not by the heart of the worshiper has received little benefit from his own custom. Why is this so hard for us? Thank God for the diversity that multiplies our witness throughout the world.—1982

FEBRUARY 14

Luke 9:23. *He said to them all, "If any want to become my followers, let them deny themselves and take up their cross daily and follow me."*

An illustration from Kierkegaard: There was once a noble horse in the prime of its life. It was five years old, a thoroughbred, and filled with fire. A comfortable old cab driver, on hearing the horse was for sale, said, "I can't use that horse. He is too frisky, too strong; he'd pull my old carriage to pieces, and make me get a new one. I don't want that horse." Eight years later the old cab driver saw the horse again, now a slow, easy-going hack. So the cab driver bought him, and the old horse fit perfectly with the old carriage. There was no need for the cab driver to change any of his comfortable ways.

This is a parable of the two kinds of Christianity in the world today. One is sleepy, easy-going, comfortable, and you won't have to change your life a bit if you come to it. It's a very "proper" thing, like going to the right school or having the right kind of silver on your table.

The other kind, the following of Christ, will mean a new carriage. You will have to get rid of prejudice, humbly serve your fellow men and women, and work for justice in your community. This second kind means that you give your life to Christ.—1943

FEBRUARY 15

Philippians 2:3. *Do nothing from selfish ambition or conceit, but in humility regard others as better than yourselves.*

Paul's focus here is sharing God's grace: the central mission of the church. Sharing in the gospel is a key point of the letter to the Philippians. "You share in God's grace," Paul tells his friends in Philippi. Where does the idea come from that you can be a Christian alone, that "me and thee, O Lord" is all that matters? It is a common heresy, and Paul would not have understood it. He bids us share the gospel message in humility.

Did you ever see a child open a wonderful present and not share it with anyone? Would a newly engaged couple keep the good news to themselves? Good news is to be shared. The gospel, as we understand it, has to be shared. Without the shared message, the power of the Word would be lost.

"I pray," says Paul, "that your love may overflow." Love is never static; it grows or it diminishes. In growth, our capacity to love breaks through, overflows, and takes root in first one person, and then another, and then another. Love is always to be shared. And in sharing the gospel message of love we are truly honoring God and our neighbor.—2001

FEBRUARY 16

Philippians 3:8. *I regard everything as loss because of the surpassing value of knowing Christ Jesus my Lord.*

Can Paul be serious in advising us to regard everything we have as so much rubbish to be lost? Our whole world seems to orbit from the energy generated by those who avoid loss at all cost. For many, it is their reason to live. But Paul understands that a relationship with Christ Jesus surpasses all earthly things.

We do much better remembering our baptismal vows. Reinhold Niebuhr, a great theologian of the twentieth century, puts it well:

Nothing worth doing is completed in our lifetime;

> *therefore, we are saved by hope.*

Nothing true or beautiful or good makes complete sense in any immediate context of history;

> *therefore, we are saved by faith.*

Nothing we do, however virtuous, can be accomplished alone;

> *therefore, we are saved by love.*

No virtuous act is quite as virtuous from the standpoint of our friend or foe as from our own;

> *therefore, we are saved by the final form of love— which is forgiveness.*—2005

FEBRUARY 17

Joel 2:12-13. *Yet even now, says the Lord, return to me with all your heart, with fasting, with weeping, and with mourning; rend your hearts and not your clothing.*

Lent begins today, and the time is ripe to remind ourselves of what it means to keep Lent. First of all, it is clearly a special season. Out of the 365 days, forty are chosen in which we are called to make a special effort.

Human nature is so made that if unseen realities, like God and the soul, are left to be attended to at just any time, in the hope that somehow they will be attended to at all times, the chances are they will not be attended to at all.

If we are to move forward, we can best do it by making special efforts at special times. Through all the year we need what Lent brings us, but we can make that discovery only by keeping Lent. Thus, like most of the church's traditions, Lent is founded on common sense, and on the deep needs of human nature.—1954

FEBRUARY 18

John 17:4-5. *I glorified you on earth by finishing the work that you gave me to do. So now, Father, glorify me in your own presence with the glory that I had in your presence before the world existed.*

Two men were walking slowly along a city street, engaged in earnest conversation. Suddenly they came face to face with an elderly woman, poorly clad and somewhat stooped. The men were startled by her appearance—not by her poverty, nor her physical weakness, but by her face. "What a beautiful face," said one. "Yes," said the other, "behind that face there is a soul, there is an inner glory which shines through every line. This woman has suffered, and it is her suffering which has wrought in her that beauty which we see."

Suffering, rightly used, develops character as nothing else does. It brings to light the glory that is within and that glory touches and wins others. So it was with our Lord. The cross revealed his glory. It showed what he was. The way we face suffering will show what we are. May it always reveal an inner glory.—1940

FEBRUARY 19

Philippians 4:8. *Beloved, whatever is true, whatever is honorable, whatever is just, whatever is pure, whatever is pleasing...if there is any excellence and if there is anything worthy of praise, think about these things.*

Anxiety is a kind of fear—not of God, but of the unknown future. It is unreality. We draw the unreal future into the present and proceed to stab ourselves with it. How passionately Jesus strove to overcome our delusion of crossing bridges before we come to them! Imagine an able and loving father whose children ran about in panic lest next year they might not have food to eat or clothes to wear.

Anxiety is a symptom. The disease is mistrust of our heavenly Father. The cure is to look around and see what he has done for us already and to thank him for it. How many lovely things, how much to praise him for! If anything is needed, ask. Then leave it to God. If he doesn't give it, so much the better. It wasn't needed. What God always will give—if we trust him—is his peace, the best gift.—1946

FEBRUARY 20

Psalm 43:3. *Send out your light and your truth, that they may lead me, and bring me to your holy hill and to your dwelling.*

At the time that the psalmist offers this prayer, he has had more than his fill of human cruelty and crookedness. He is sick of human ways, and longs for a closer walk with God.

We recognize in this psalm a familiar experience. It is that the evil in the world around us somehow makes us feel far from God. Why should our neighbor's ungodliness be a wedge between God and us? This is a mystery, although we realize that our neighbor's sin is not solely his own; we are involved in it too. Just as my sin is yours, and the whole world's, we are all bound together in the sin of the world.

The sin that alienates our neighbor from God has the same power to alienate us from God. Whatever the full explanation, it is out of the depths of the world's sin and separation from God that every soul must cry to him: "Send out your light and your truth, that they may lead me, and bring me to your holy hill and to your dwelling." In returning to God, in following his light to his sanctuary, in worshiping him, we find restoration and healing and his "saving health."—1957

FEBRUARY 21

Luke 4:1, 2. *Jesus, full of the Holy Spirit...was led by the Spirit in the wilderness, where for forty days he was tempted by the devil.*

Scripture tells us Jesus was full of the Holy Spirit during the wilderness experience. God had seen to it that Jesus was alive in a way he had never been before—healthy, filled with the Spirit, a new dimension of relationship developing and being revealed to him. He went into the desert whole and complete, in faithful obedience. And he went into that wilderness because he was led by the Spirit to go there—he was not banished, exiled, driven out. He went accompanied by God, led by God, filled by God.

We are never alone in our trips into the desert. We are filled with the Spirit ourselves and led by the Spirit. Accompanied, filled with love and God, we understand clearly that relationship with God is everything.

Next time you are led into the desert, or the first time, remember that you are filled with the Spirit and that the Spirit is leading you. The devil will talk on, but your spirit will listen and respond only to God.—1992

FEBRUARY 22

Mark 1:1. *The beginning of the good news of Jesus Christ, the Son of God.*

Before the gospel records were put into writing, there existed an oral tradition in the churches. Parts of the gospels seem to have been recited—especially the sayings of Jesus—during gatherings for worship. At some point—probably soon after a great fire in Rome—a man called Mark was moved to put the mighty works of God into a short story.

Thus, by the year 65 C.E. we have documented evidence written during the lifetime of some of the witnesses of the events described. These stated facts could have been challenged: the fact that they were not attests to their truth, however strange and mysterious it may seem at times.

The term "gospel of Jesus Christ" means the good news about our human salvation because of the life, death, and resurrection of Jesus; it means the good news as taught and proclaimed by Jesus. In Mark's account there is a great sense of urgency revealed in a leader keen to bring God's saving grace quickly into the world—while there is yet time.—1966

FEBRUARY 23

1 Corinthians 1:28-29. *God chose what is low and despised in the world, things that are not, to reduce to nothing things that are, so that no one might boast in the presence of God.*

He did. God chose some pretty dubious characters to spread his message. Slaves, prisoners, crazies, a long-haired, locust-eating man, and a gang of roguish fishermen led by a radical, left-wing carpenter. Being a long-haired, slightly crazy, radical prison inmate, I feel at home among that crowd.

A few years ago, I wrote a series of these meditations. Before I began, I was worried that people would shut me out—despise me because I was lowly—and miss the message. They didn't, far from it. They carried a very powerful message back to me. So, again, I ask: please don't shut out the message.

I know, on the surface, it doesn't make sense that God would use such unlikely people to carry this most important message. But when I realize what the message is, it dawns on me that no one would know more about it than those in dire need of it. The experts. It makes perfect sense when you consider the message.

The message? Love. The messenger? You. You're in good company.—1998

FEBRUARY 24

John 15:7-8. *If you abide in me…you bear much fruit and become my disciples.*

Jesus' teaching was effective because he used everyday examples. Even to this day many of the hills of Israel are covered with vineyards. Those who heard Jesus knew what he was talking about when he mentioned vines and branches and pruning and bearing fruit.

This image of Jesus as the true vine was a vivid teaching for the people of his time. They knew full well what happened to branches that were separated from the vine. They did not bear fruit. They withered and died and were thrown into the fire and burnt.

This is the important teaching of this passage. Branches simply cannot bear fruit if they are separated from the vine. Jesus is the vine and the disciples are the branches. Their ministry cannot be effective, cannot bear fruit, cannot even exist unless they are connected to the source and power of their ministry, Jesus Christ. There can only be an effective fruit-bearing ministry for the disciples—and for us—if it is grounded in Christ: only if we dwell in him as he dwells in us. Our ministry can only exist in this living union with Christ.—1981

FEBRUARY 25

Psalm 19:7-8. *The law of the Lord is perfect and revives the soul; the testimony of the Lord is sure and gives wisdom to the innocent. The statutes of the Lord are just and rejoice the heart; the commandment of the Lord is clear and gives light to the eyes.*

Law is the product of an intelligence other than humanity's. As Lord Balfour noted, it is unthinkable that certain electrons have assembled themselves and finally produced the minds of men and women, and that their minds can then analyze the nonintelligent forces that created them.

The order of the planets, the order in nature, the order in our physical bodies, could not possibly be the result of chance. Law and order in the physical universe demand an intelligence to create them if they demand an intelligence to appreciate them. A human mind could not be superior to the author of the universe.

The observance and the analysis of these laws enable us to have a science which assumes that there is an ordered universe. If things had sprung from chance there could be no science, because there would be no certainty that a given cause would give a dependable result. When the laws discovered by science are broken, the result is sure to be disastrous to life.

Incline our hearts, O Lord, to keep thy law.—1937

FEBRUARY 26

Mark 2:21. *No one sews a piece of unshrunk cloth on an old cloak; otherwise, the patch pulls away from it, the new from the old, and a worse tear is made.*

With this simple sentence Jesus helps us confront the enigma of the old and the new. Jesus does not say the new is better, but that because it has not yet shrunk— has not been broken in, as it were—it will not repair the rip but make the situation worse. Nor does Jesus say that the old is no longer worth using and must be discarded. So the solution is to make the new cloth compatible with the old before utilizing it.

Can we apply that to our lives and to our faith? Our Christian faith does not begin with Jesus. It begins with the faith he inherited. What we find new in Jesus' words was often not new in his own community; it is new to us only because we are ignorant of that faith. So let us learn how to treasure that older but still usable cloth—Judaism—and then see how our new cloth can be accommodated to it, so that the tear which tore apart the fabric of faith long ago may be mended.—1990

FEBRUARY 27

1 Corinthians 4:6. *That you may learn through us the meaning of the saying, "Nothing beyond what is written," so that none of you will be puffed up in favor of one against another.*

Humility is a strange and wonderful thing in the life of any Christian. But how do you prove that you are humble? Should you even try to get credit for humility? We sometimes see people who belittle themselves so much that they evoke the opposite response: they seem to be proud of their lack of pride!

Love is the only root that bears humility upon its branches. To see and ever to be mindful of the needs and conditions of others is the first step leading toward humility. To help meet these needs is to put into operation the spirit of the true Christian servant.

To make oneself a mat upon which others may walk at will is not being humble. Rather, it is placing self in the limelight for attention, hoping to bring notice to the act of self-abasement. Being humble is not cutting yourself down to smaller stature. It is standing to the fullness of your height in God's presence, without forgetting how small you really are.—1960

FEBRUARY 28

Psalm 27:15. *Show me your way, O LORD.*

We can't escape from paradox when we think about God. We must try not to forget that while God never ceases to work in his universe and in us, he also never ceases to rest. Relaxation and leisure are all part of the divine energy, forever creating, forever renewing, and forever at peace within God. We do well to take note of this. For, in our fussing and busyness, we must occasionally stand still; and God tells us to do so. "Be still, and know that I am God."

The busier we get the more indispensable we imagine ourselves to be, and we end up having exhausted ourselves to death and having bored our brothers to death with the clatter and clamor of it all. One of the greatest Christian leaders in this generation can often be found by one of his staff just sitting, thinking. Not writing, not dictating, not organizing, not interviewing—just sitting. From those periods of peace amid a killingly busy life emerge wise words, written, preached, acted upon. The work gets done, and done more keenly, more coolly.

Resting in the Lord is a form of prayer we must learn in order to really enjoy spiritual maturity. God's will is our peace for the very reason that it is his serene wisdom making itself felt in our lives. Be strong, take courage, and wait for the Lord.—1974

FEBRUARY 29

Psalm 4:8. *I lie down in peace; at once I fall asleep; for only you, LORD, make me dwell in safety.*

This psalm is often said at Compline. Compline, also called "Night Prayer," is the daily office said before sleep. In our community we sometimes jokingly refer to it as "Good night, God." Its opening words, "The Lord Almighty grant us a peaceful night and a perfect end," often start off instinctive yawns.

In the monastery, the daily offices shape our life together. Compline is prayer for God's blessing, protection, and peace as we sleep. Most of us feel safe in our sleep, but for some the night brings terrors—those living with violence, those struggling with addictions or with terminal or painful illnesses, those with difficult domestic relationships, those who fear natural disasters, and so on.

Modern comforts dull our sensitivity during the day, but the darkness exposes the raw power of our fears. In our prayers let us remember all who struggle through the night. If you do not do so already, you might find it helpful to say Compline.—2010

MARCH

FORWARD
day by day

1957 · SUMMER

MARCH 1

Psalm 57:9. *I will confess you among the peoples, O Lord; I will sing praise to you among the nations.*

Some of the idioms of the Psalter must be explained. "Peoples" and "nations" mean Gentiles, outsiders, uncircumcised, irreligious, pagan. Those of us who are anxious over the increasing secularity of our society are more comfortable in a religious atmosphere, where the Bible is read in schools and God is honored in the fabric of our total society. Another psalmist faces the fact that to live in a totally secular society is treachery to God: "How shall we sing the Lord's song upon an alien soil?" (Psalm 137:4).

Today's psalmist, though, emphasizes the opposite side of the coin. In the midst of those who deny God, in the secular society and in the secular city, it is still possible to serve him. Our job is still to waken the dawn and to confess the Lord among the peoples, to sing to him among those who know him not.—1967

MARCH 2

Mark 3:32-35. *A crowd was sitting around him; and they said to him, "Your mother and your brothers and sisters are outside, asking for you." And he replied, "Who are my mother and my brothers?" And looking at those who sat around him, he said, "Here are my mother and my brothers! Whoever does the will of God is my brother and sister and mother."*

Perhaps verses 20 and 21, with their reference to his family's attempt to restrain Jesus, belong here. Did Jesus' friends bring blessed Mary from Nazareth upon the report that Jesus was losing his mind?

Had the scribes been whispering in Nazareth in the hope that the mother would fetch him home and silence him? He had always been so good to her. But Jesus refuses to let blood kinship limit love kinship. He offers himself as brother to any who do God's will.

That offer holds good today, no matter who you are or what you have been.

God comes first. His claim is prior even to a mother's or a motherland's. There is defeat in store for any nation which teaches its children that it is right to hate a brother race, or to claim from its citizens that worship and allegiance which belongs alone to God. —1936

MARCH 3

Mark 4:8. *Other seed fell into good soil and brought forth grain, growing up and increasing and yielding thirty and sixty and a hundredfold.*

This is the beginning of Mark's chapter of parables, revealing Jesus' teaching rather than his mighty deeds. The parable of the sower is the most familiar. We are surprised, therefore, that it is explained so carefully. This may reflect an interpretation of Jesus' thought rather than the actual teaching, although Mark does say in verse 34 that Jesus explained his parables later to his disciples. The emphasis is on the importance of attentive listening.

Surely in all good teaching all members of an audience get what they are equipped to receive, and Jesus would seem to encourage this, as he appears to in verses 10-12. How attentive are we to his message? How much do we get from it? Have we still deficiencies in the art of good listening? Do we do something about it? What is the good fruit we have borne?—1966

MARCH 4

Mark 4:26-27. *The kingdom of God is as if someone would scatter seed on the ground, and would sleep and rise night and day, and the seed would sprout and grow, he does not know how.*

So that is the kingdom of God? I've always wondered. Is it the kingdom of heaven? In Matthew (in the camel and eye of the needle story), Jesus talks about the two as though they are the same. As soon as the word heaven appears, I think fluffy clouds, ivory mansions, and gold streets. That's a wonderful ideal, but I need my meat and potatoes. Sometimes, my faith is pretty watery and I want to say, "What about right now?" I want to be able to touch that kingdom.

Jesus gives us that here. First of all, it's something we can comprehend. A person. A seed. Grain. Growing and maturing. Yeah, that's painting a simple enough picture. Ground. Night and day. A person sleeping, getting up, yawning, stretching, starting the day. Soil. I can touch that stuff.

This isn't up in the sky, some abstract vision conjured up by someone too holy to communicate with me. It's Jesus, and he's talking about things on the ground. Right now. Today. This very real moment. You. Me.

The kingdom. It is here. Welcome.—1998

MARCH 5

Mark 4:40. *Why are you afraid? Have you still no faith?*

We have all experienced that following Christ does not exempt us from storms. In fact it is in the "storms" that we experience the reality of Christ's presence and power and receive lessons we would never otherwise learn.

Our problem is our memories. The disciples, in the middle of today's gale force winds and towering waves that threaten to sink the boat, forget yesterday's miracles. They forget that the same Master who performed miracles is with them in the boat. Fear is the most irrational of emotions, and it is fear that fills their minds. Moreover, they imagine that the Jesus who showed such compassion yesterday has changed his character today, and has ceased to care.

Having calmed the sea, Jesus gently shows them that fear and faith are incompatible. Strangely, it is faith that is the more rational of the two. We need to remember that this same Jesus lives today, as our High Priest. He is still sympathetic to our weakness, patient with our faithlessness, and mighty in his power.—1982

MARCH 6

Mark 5:2. *And when he had stepped out of the boat, immediately a man out of the tombs with an unclean spirit met him.*

As Jesus steps out of the boat, a crazy man rushes toward him, jumping, shrieking, waving his arms. To the disciples he is a loathsome menace to be over-powered or fled from. But Jesus sees past the filth and ravings. He sees a suffering child of God. His whole being goes forth in a mighty wave of pity, trying to penetrate the frightful exterior. His only thought is to help. That is love in action; Christ coming to the outcast.

You may have some repulsive disease; you may be disgusted at your sin; others may have imprisoned you as a threat to their safety; because of your color they may treat you as only partly human; you may live in poverty or squalor; your mind may be unsteady. But Christ sees in you one who can become a strong, useful child of God. He offers you his friendship, his power, his love, a share in his work. Will you accept it? Will you believe in yourself as Christ does and let his companionship make you what you might be?—1936

MARCH 7

1 Corinthians 10:13. *No testing has overtaken you that is not common to everyone...with the testing [God] will also provide the way out so that you may be able to endure it.*

"I can't stand the pressure. I have to describe our product as the boss says, but I know it's not true," a young salesman told a friend.

Two weeks later they met again. The salesman said, "I thought about Christ in Gethsemane. It looked as though death would end all his work. He must have felt that for the sake of the kingdom of God he had to live on, and he knew he could still escape. It was a decision between right and wrong. He prayed until he knew what was right, then did it in spite of the cross. Peter, in his temptation, didn't pray, so he denied his Master in the pinch.

"Well, I figured I had better try our Lord's way if I were going to call myself a Christian. So I thought through my problems on my knees until I knew what was right; and then I prayed until I wanted to do it. Today I told the boss I was going to tell the truth, and if he didn't like it he could fire me, and I would make my way somehow." —1936

MARCH 8

Mark 5:36. *But overhearing what they said, Jesus said to the leader of the synagogue, "Do not fear, only believe."*

When they interview notable subjects, reporters often first ask silly questions because it is hard to start the visitors talking.

Similarly, it would be silly to ask a great Bible scholar, "What is the greatest word in the Bible?"

Yet it is not an altogether idle question, for one great Bible scholar, Bishop B. F. Westcott, records a visit to his old schoolmaster, Bishop Prince Lee, who said: "People quote various words of the Lord as containing the sum of the gospel—the Lord's Prayer, the Sermon on the Mount, and the like. To me the essence of the gospel is in simpler and shorter terms: Be not afraid, only believe. Ah! Westcott, mark that only." Lee's eyes filled with tears as he said this.

The opposite of belief is not unbelief; it is fear. Mark that only! Fear of loss, fear of death, fear of consequences, fear of unpopularity, of neighbors' opinions. We have our intellectual difficulties, but deeper than that is lack of courage.—1942

MARCH 9

Genesis 45:4. *Then Joseph said to his brothers, "Come closer to me." And they came closer. He said, "I am your brother, Joseph, whom you sold into Egypt."*

Joseph speaks of his life as Pharaoh's son and how God intended him to be there to preserve life through the years of famine. Having told them the truth, he kisses all his brothers and weeps upon them; and after that his brothers talk with him.

Until this moment, the brothers are silent. Then they talk to Joseph. The harsh wrong they have done to Joseph cannot be undone. Nothing Joseph says changes the past. The turning point in the story happens only after the one who has been betrayed speaks and forgives. Only then do they talk.

Reconciliation often waits out the tongue-tied guilty who will not or cannot speak first. Why must words of forgiveness precede confession of guilt and remorse? That seems unfair. But if starting over depends only upon justice, where would we be? If new beginnings require confession before being forgiven, who can be healed? Who in your life stands in guilty silence waiting for you to speak? What reconciliation depends upon your decision to be the first to draw closer and to weep?—2006

MARCH 10

Romans 8:14. *For all who are led by the Spirit of God are children of God.*

The apostle Paul writes that we "have received a spirit of adoption," and as such are like Christ—we are heirs of God. There is no difference in the love God has for us and for Jesus, the Son of God. We are all God's children.

In the United States adoption is common. A great phenomenon of our time is the number of international adoptions. Amid the variety of ways children come to have parents, one truth prevails among the families I know—the parents love their children, and it makes no difference how the children entered the family.

It is like this with God, who adopts us. Each one of us is special to God, who loves us. God's Spirit brings us together, transforms us, and unites us. Because we are members of the divine family, the Spirit of God leads us out of slavery and fear. If we suffer with Christ then we will also experience the glory of resurrection. We can call God our Father, and we can call Jesus our brother. God's unconditional love is the bond that holds our special family together and teaches us to grow.—2012

MARCH 11

Mark 6:46. *After saying farewell to them, he went up on the mountain to pray.*

In this chapter of Mark, Jesus learns about John the Baptist's terrible murder, finds a lonely place apart to collect himself, and then tackles the teaching and feeding of five thousand persons. Mark depicts an active, can-do Jesus, but we also see one who prays every chance he gets.

Prayer is unlike vitamins or exercise—it is impossible to overdose! Brother Lawrence, a 17th century monk, prayed joyfully as he washed dishes. A rancher friend of mine prays as he spends hours alone in the saddle. Richard Foster, the Quaker writer and teacher, has joined a covenant of friends who take five minutes at noon to stop every other activity, assess how their morning has gone, and ask God's continual guidance.

Perhaps you can experiment with some new ways of praying. You might try a short prayer of thanksgiving for every person with whom you speak in a given day. Or you might offer a stoplight prayer: "You are patience and joy, O God. Help me be more like you."

Saint Teresa of Avila said: "There is but one road that reaches God, and that is prayer. If anyone shows you another, you are being deceived."—1992

MARCH 12

1 Corinthians 9:22. *I have become all things to all people, that I might by all means save some.*

"Son, remember who you are." My dad's frequent advice accompanied me on my first day of school, my first date, first job, first day in prison. For a long time, the depth of his advice went right over my head. Remembering who I am is an intricate part of following Paul's advice—basically, don't say one thing and do another.

Most of my life, I've been pretty insecure about who I am, and consequently have spent my energy trying to impress others and present my continuously updated, what-I-think-will-make-me-acceptable-in-your-eyes image of myself. In learning what my beliefs are and how to live in tune with them, I am slowly coming to know that God loves me. That knowledge empowers me to be who I am, not who I think everyone else wants me to be.

If you've spent your life wondering who you are, finally being comfortable in your own skin is quite a gift. Attraction is much more effective than promotion. We do have a message. What we do, not what we say, will spread it.—1998

MARCH 13

Mark 7:5. *Why do your disciples not live according to the tradition of the elders?*

This question, raised by the guardians of religious orthodoxy, highlights a growing tension between Jesus and the "Institution." His ministry was conditioned by compassion and an openness to the possibility that rules can change. Jesus fully supported and observed the principles on which faith was based, but rejected the minutia of regulations which enslaved people. He was constantly dealing with the question of what must remain and what must be relinquished in the tradition.

We all tend to cling to what is familiar and fear the newness that invites change. A new prayer book, a different minister, or children whose values challenge ours can be painful catalysts for our faith. Letting go is a vital part of growth in the natural world and in our spiritual quest, and grasping at the past can become a form of idolatry. Today's reading is an invitation to ponder the question: What do I really need to retain from the past as I embrace the present and move toward the future?—1989

MARCH 14

Luke 15:20. *But while he was still far off, his father saw him and was filled with compassion; he ran and put his arms around him and kissed him.*

One New Year's Eve our son begged to go to a friend's house. He had just started skateboarding and was making new friends, some of whom we did not know. It was a trying time. He was to be home by 9 p.m. Nine o'clock came and went, and he didn't come home. We called the number he had left; there was no answer. We waited. We prayed. We fretted.

Finally, he called. "Can you come pick me up?" "Where are you?" "I don't know." He tried to describe the intersection. It could have been one of two dozen in the city. He was on the other side of town. I got into the car with my cell phone and headed out. It started to sleet. Traffic was horrible. I couldn't find him. I drove, called home, and drove some more. Then, by chance, I turned around in a fast-food restaurant parking lot and there he was, huddled under the awning trying to stay dry. He got in the car but flinched as I turned to him. I was angry. But I looked into his eyes and saw how alone, cold, and afraid he was. "I'm so happy that you are safe," I said. We both cried. "Come on, let's go home." I had often read the story of the Prodigal Son, but I never really understood it until that night.—2002

MARCH 15

Mark 7:34. *Then looking up to heaven, he sighed and said to him, "Ephphatha," that is, "Be opened."*

Anthony Bloom, archbishop of the Eastern Orthodox Church in England, records that one of the first people to seek his advice after his ordination was an elderly lady. "I have been praying almost unceasingly for fourteen years," she said, "and I have never had any sense of God's presence." It appeared that her prayer times were filled with her talking, so Anthony Bloom suggested that she set apart fifteen minutes a day to "sit and just knit before the face of God." The woman later reported that when she talked to God she felt nothing, but when she sat quietly she felt wrapped in his presence.

When we wish that we had more recorded prayers of Jesus, it may be that we too regard prayer predominantly as conversation. In today's reading, Jesus is not in solitude but fully engaged at the point of human need. Prayer consisted of a look toward heaven and a sigh. Maybe there was no time for more than this. But could it be that even on the lonely hillsides Jesus often simply looked toward his Father, and the uplifted spirit was the prayer? Prayer can be a trustful waiting, a single word or sentence, a look of hope.—1975

MARCH 16

Isaiah 30:18-19. *For the L*ORD *is a God of justice; blessed are all who who wait for him...you shall weep no more.*

A continuing debate in South Africa is whether apartheid still holds power over its people. Freedom officially arrived in 1994 with the first democratic elections and the onset of the wide-ranging Truth and Reconciliation hearings. Some argue that the country should no longer use apartheid as an excuse for inadequate service delivery and mediocre leadership. Others believe South Africa's people and systems are still deeply affected by the racist oppression of the apartheid years.

We visited a school in a township of Grahamstown. A lawyer told us about his role in defending students who had been arrested after protesting conditions at their school under apartheid. As we looked at the playground where the students had gathered, we began to sense the injustice they faced, the courage they showed, and the fear they must have felt.

The God of justice has surely been with the people of this country. But many, who live in poverty and carry the scars of the oppressed, are waiting for a time when they will weep no more. —2014

MARCH 17

1 Corinthians 12:7. *To each is given the manifestation of the Spirit for the common good.*

Christianity proclaims the God of all people and "of all things visible and invisible." He is the God of the Hindu, the atheist, the communist, the fascist, the humanist, and the garden variety agnostic, just as much as he is the God of an assorted variety of Jews and Christians. He is the One Unchanging Reality in a universe whose only constant is change. God is near us when we feel lost, just as he is near us when we are aware of his presence. We would not know to feel lost, were we totally unaware of his presence. People in the world would not know they are separated if it were not for our basic unity in God. God is real whether or not people have in their minds an idea that there is a God, whatever their notions about his nature.

A constant danger for Christians is that we may lose awareness of God's loving and redemptive power in the world. When we do this, we lose our mission to proclaim and to reveal or disclose the nearness of the kingdom of heaven to every person. We lose our apostolic mission and begin to judge others by how much they are like ourselves. When we cannot see manifestations of the Spirit in our brothers and sisters, we become spiritually impoverished.—1966

MARCH 18

1 Corinthians 12:12. *For just as the body is one and has many members, and all the members of the body, though many, are one body, so it is with Christ.*

Watching an orchestra, I noticed three things. First, the unchangeable oboe sounded the pitch and all the other players tuned to it. Second, the musicians each concentrated on their own instrument. Third, they watched the written score before them but played according to the interpretation of the conductor. What a fine parable for the church!

Composers writing for an orchestra don't want a hundred clarinets. They call for families of varying voices, in groups both large and small—all playing in harmony. In the church it doesn't matter whether all think alike, but that we love one another, find our own faults rather than our neighbor's, be in tune with the congregation, and follow the score as directed by our conductor.

We must practice alone, but in a concert only one score can be played at a time. Someone must arrange the program if the church is to produce harmony and not discord. Let us keep the unity of the Spirit in the bond of peace, rather than the uniformity of our opinions in the bond of prejudice.—1937

MARCH 19

Psalm 89:5. *The heavens bear witness to your wonders, O Lᴏʀᴅ, and to your faithfulness in the assembly of the holy ones.*

I recall as a child gazing up at the Milky Way one night. I sensed the wonder and grandeur of God, surrounded by heavenly beings who praised and served him. Years later, after lots of education, I still marveled at the Milky Way, but I wasn't so sure about God, and the thought of heavenly beings had come to seem a bit foolish.

Children may be on to something. They don't assume as much as adults do. Adults want verification before they believe; they assume if something is real, they must be able to find it, measure it, and analyze it. This eliminates fairies, guardian angels, the devil, and God. What a dull universe! Children, on the other hand, believe in things invisible and unknowable. Their universe includes mystery and wonder.

Joseph and Mary responded to a reality invisible and unknowable. By startling choice and miraculous design, this reality assumed an additional nature and so became visible and known. An "assembly of the holy ones" also appeared, in a field. A star is said to have borne witness to the event. When you hear the story, if you don't quite get it, ask a child.—2001

MARCH 20

Mark 9:29. *This kind can come out only through prayer.*

I can identify with the disciples. The disciples had tried, no doubt with the best intentions, to cast out an unclean spirit, but they had failed. We, too, often fired with enthusiasm, try to do God's work only to fail. A stewardship drive, an adult Bible class, introducing a newcomer to Christ—any number of projects on which we embark can fall surprisingly flat, leaving us wondering why. When we have a brilliant idea for some project for God, amazed at our own ingenuity, do we pray about it? When we venture to "go out on a limb" for God, impressed with our own courage, do we pray about it? When we endeavor to reach or help others for God, pleased with our own magnanimity, do we pray about it? Or do we assume everything depends on our own talent, energy, intelligence, and leadership?

Jesus said, "Apart from me you can do nothing" (John 15:5). In my experience, I can actually do a lot of things on my own, but I have discovered that in the end, none of them matters. What matters is what Jesus does through me, and that happens only when I have surrendered my will to him and gotten out of the way.—1979

MARCH 21

Philippians 3:13-14. *One thing I do: forgetting what lies behind and straining forward to what lies ahead, I press on toward the goal for the prize of the heavenly call of God in Christ Jesus.*

Memories constitute an important part of who we are. Relish the good ones and never forget them. Some memories we hold in common; some are unique just for us. For me, my wedding day; the power of the Holy Spirit and the pressure of all the hands on my head at my ordination to the priesthood; the joy and wonder of the births of my children (I was lucky to experience what many men formerly were not allowed to witness); watching the sun set into the ocean from a promontory in the Azores—in a perfectly cloudless sky so it appeared to be sinking directly into the Atlantic.

I am certain that in today's passage Paul is inviting us to dis-remember the bad things we have said and done and experienced. Notice how closely the words "forgive" and "forget" are intertwined in our language. If we fail to let go of a past that haunts us, allowing ourselves to be paralyzed by guilt or pain, we shall not be able to press on for the "heavenly call of God in Christ." Repent and forget the bad stuff. Then move on, sharing the Good News of Jesus Christ. —2005

MARCH 22

Exodus 4:12. *Now go, and I will be with your mouth and teach you what you are to speak.*

This chapter in Exodus gives us the four voices in which Moses could speak to Israel and to Pharaoh, the same voices we have been using ever since. The first is symbolized by the rod become snake. This is the way of force and fear. People can be frightened into obedience by the show of power.

The second voice is that of mystery and magic. Moses, in making his hand leprous at will, appealed to magic. This is the promise of a panacea to cure all ills. We look for it in technology and politics; wonder drugs are not confined to medicine.

The third voice is that of authority, illustrated by Aaron the priest. The appeal here is to tradition. At best it is second-hand and derived. For all its impressive rite and ceremony, the power sometimes goes out of it.

The only satisfactory appeal is through our own personal experience and witness. Like Moses, we may seem to be slow of speech, but we cannot foist our task off on any Aaron. We dare not say, "Send some other person." Not by the voice of force, magic, or authority, but only in the voice of personal concern and commitment will the message be heard.—1971

MARCH 23

Psalm 122:1. *"Let us go to the house of the Lord."*

Garrison Keillor, chronicler of Lake Wobegon, was raised in the Plymouth Brethren Church, whose services are quite simple. Back in small-town Minnesota, their picture of Episcopalians was "wealthy people, Yale graduates, worshiping God in extremely good taste. Episcopalian was the church in wingtips, the church of Scotch and soda," Keillor writes in *We Are Still Married.*

Then he discovered Holy Apostles Church in New York, a little congregation worshiping in a run-down building, with all kinds of people, and running a soup kitchen that fed a thousand New Yorkers every day. Though he had trouble juggling Prayer Book, hymnal, and bulletin, "I felt glad to be there. When we stood for prayers, bringing slowly to mind the goodness and the poverty of our lives, the lives of others, the life to come, it brought tears to your eyes, the simple way the Episcopalians pray."

I want to remember what he wrote. When next I get angry or frustrated about our endless arguing over who's righteous and who's not, I want to remember that I am glad when I go into the house of the Lord and join in "the simple way the Episcopalians pray."—1991

MARCH 24

Mark 10:14. *Let the little children come to me; do not stop them.*

"Whatever my sins may be," says Mr. Average Contemporary Christian, "the last thing I would dream of doing would be to stop any child from coming to Christ." This is easily said, even easily believed. But we watched a TV documentary the other evening on juvenile delinquency. So many of the things we cheerfully put up with—slums, poverty, social neglect, racial and ethnic ghettos—do stop children from coming to the Lord of life. All this is in our own land. In other lands, millions of children live in desperate poverty, with none to give them either the Bread of Life or daily bread for their bodies. Of course you and I do nothing actively to stop any child, or anybody else, from coming to Christ. But we may do so, nevertheless, effectively by our neglect, by our leaving undone the things we ought to do to make this a better world for all children.

We Americans easily go into sentimental raptures about children: how we love them all! But the Lord who calls all children to himself demands more than empty sentimentalism from us.—1965

MARCH 25

Luke 1:38. *Then Mary said, "Here am I, the servant of the Lord; let it be with me according to your word."*

What would your answer have been? I probably would have said, "That's a fantastic idea, Mr. Angel, but if we do it your way, I'll miss working out tomorrow. Also, I had plans for this weekend. It's not that I don't want to, it's just that, well, you know, I'm pretty busy. So could we do it my way?"

I have recently felt more at peace than I've ever felt before. I'm also happier than I've ever been. Healthier. Most free. Most successful. Most grateful. I think I'm starting to realize God's will in my life, accepting that God wants good for me. Thing is, I wouldn't have picked this route. I would have chosen an easier, softer way. I now know there was no other path for me except the one I've walked.

Every wrong choice, mistake, and painful moment has been a step in this journey. For this reason, my prayer these days is:

God. Whatever. Thank you.

It's not a foot-dragging, whining whatever. It's a whatever from a person who is beginning to realize that God has a bigger and better plan than he does. Mary said the same thing.—1965

MARCH 26

2 Corinthians 4:3-4. *And even if our gospel is veiled, it is veiled to those who are perishing. In their case the god of this world has blinded the minds of the unbelievers, to keep them from seeing the light of the gospel of the glory of Christ, who is the image of God.*

A teacher stopped suddenly and turned upon the class with the question: "What is good about the Good News?" We stammered and hemmed and hawed. The goodness of the gospel can be veiled.

Water is good to the thirsty. Bread is good to the hungry. Relief is good to the sufferer. Freedom is good to the prisoner. Love is good to the lonely. Deliverance is good to the perishing. But to whom is the gospel good?

Here is the main work of the church. We must make known the Good News. We must realize that people are thirsty, hungry, in pain, imprisoned, lonely, perishing. Christ says, "This is the work of God, that you believe in him whom he has sent" (John 6:29). The moment we believe, we recognize how good is the gospel. When we have what is good, we want to give it to others. We preach by word, act, and life. "For we do not proclaim ourselves; we proclaim Jesus Christ as Lord" (2 Corinthians 4:5).—1941

MARCH 27

2 Corinthians 4:16, 18. *So we do not lose heart. Even though our outer nature is wasting away, our inner nature is being renewed day by day... because we look not at what can be seen but at what cannot be seen; for what can be seen is temporary, but what cannot be seen is eternal.*

We may not like to think of it, but time is slowly taking its toll on us, and we cannot hold it at bay. We attempt all sorts of ways of trying to keep young, and especially to look young. We struggle to defeat the years by artificial tricks which do sometimes deceive our neighbors, occasionally even ourselves. But we don't really deceive ourselves: we know well enough what the truth is.

Yet here Saint Paul declares exultingly that he has found a way to defeat the years, that he has the secret of perpetual youth. The body gets older, but the spirit remains young. Time has no meaning, for he is not living in time. He has learned to live above it, to see beyond it. The eternal does not change, does not grow old, and Paul has found himself partaking of the eternal by constantly keeping his eyes on it. This is, of course, the doctrine of the whole New Testament—eternal life in the midst of time. "Those who believe in me, even though they die, will live" (John 11:25).—1945

MARCH 28

Philippians 2:5-8. *Let the same mind be in you that was in Christ Jesus, who...emptied himself, taking the form of a slave, being born in human likeness. And being found in human form, he humbled himself and became obedient to the point of death—even death on a cross.*

God in Christ has come near to us.

The German theologians, under the pressure of persecution, have been rediscovering the gospel and speak in this same language. One of them, Emil Brunner, has expressed it in these words: "It pleased God in his mercy to throw a bridge across the chasm between himself and us, to blaze a trail where we ourselves could not go. It pleased God to visit us who cannot come to God."

Notice the language used—a bridge, a trail, a visit. The gospel is a bridge thrown across the great gulf that divides God and humanity, God in his holiness and we in our sin. The gospel is a trail blazed through the undiscovered wilderness. The gospel is the visit paid by God to his people. God has come across the eternities into time. "He has visited and redeemed his people" (Luke 1:68, KJV). He did not send. He came. God in Christ has come near to us.—1948

MARCH 29

John 12:8. *You do not always have me.*

How frightening are the demands Jesus makes of us! There is no halfway when we respond to the call of Jesus. The call is to total discipleship and service. Today when we speak of giving, we mean a monetary policy; we practice stewardship, we tithe. But when we talk of Jesus giving himself, we mean he gave himself totally, even to death.

Jesus calls on his would-be followers to sell all and follow him. Have you property? Two cars? A family? Something valued more than property—your life? Can even our devotion to the poor keep us from serving the Lord?

Martha waited on Jesus at the table. Mary anointed him with an expensive ointment. Both Martha and Mary gave Jesus what was of great value: service and worship (which are the same word in Greek). Through unselfish service and constant worship, the presence of the Lord is acknowledged. The Christian is called to serve and worship the living God. Jesus is "the pioneer and perfecter of our faith, who for the sake of the joy that was set before him endured the cross, disregarding its shame, and has taken his seat at the right hand of the throne of God" (Hebrews 12:2).—1980

MARCH 30

James 1:19-20. *You must understand this, my beloved: let everyone be quick to listen, slow to speak, slow to anger; for your anger does not produce God's righteousness.*

Sure, James was writing to the Jewish Christians in the Diaspora, but he might as well have been sending a missive to parents of teens. The sleepless nights of caring for a baby, the crazed days of chasing a toddler…those we are prepared for. The whiplash emotions of a teenager? Not so much.

Those of us who are in the midst of raising teenagers would do well to heed these words from James: to be quick to listen, slow to speak, and slower still to anger. We might find that if we can abide by these words from James, it becomes as if our ears are on a pulley line to our hearts: When we open ears to hear, the heart opens too. It is a good lesson as we move through the parenting of challenging, independent, and precious teens—and an even more important one for our journey of faith.

James calls the early church—and all of us today—to hear what God is saying to us. To be changed and transformed so that we, as children of God, might be brought into nearer relationship with God the Father.—2016

MARCH 31
John 13:26. *So when he had dipped the piece of bread, he gave it to Judas son of Simon Iscariot.*

Feeding others is as intimate and as profoundly loving as washing them. To feed someone demonstrates our interdependence and need for each other. It is something that always moves me—to feed a baby, or someone sick, to pass the bread at eucharist. Feeding others is holy and good. Jesus fed the one who would betray him.

It is important for me to recognize the Judas in myself. I am a betrayer, as surely as he was. I too turn against those who love me and hurt them. More often than not, my betrayal is disguised as an act of affection. Betraying with a kiss is the way it usually goes.

There is a Judas in me. When Christ feeds me, he feeds all of me—the sinner and the saint alike. He feeds my Judas. He loves even that part of me. He loves "the least of these" in me. He loves the parts of me I hide from the world and deny. That is a remarkable feeding. He does not withold anything—even his body and his blood—from such a one as I.—1984

APRIL

Lent 1967

FORWARD
Day by Day

APRIL 1

John 13:15. *I have set you an example.*

Contrary to our usual belief, Maundy Thursday does not get its name from the institution of the Last Supper. Rather it refers to the command of love which Jesus gave to his disciples (John 15:12-17), and which he acted out for them as he washed their feet.

John's Gospel is the only one which omits any reference to the institution of the eucharist, but puts in its place this demonstration of humble service. Normally the lowliest slave in the household would be given this task. By taking it on himself, Jesus dramatizes the place of service. James and John had desired the positions of honor on his right hand and his left, but Jesus made his own place of honor as he ministered to the group. Jesus was always going off, doing the unexpected.

A feeling of oneness and concern for people characterized the life of Jesus and the Christian church during those early centuries, but even the first apostles had to learn that at the table of Christ there is no right or left hand, no head table. The communion of Christ is a circle where all people gather around on the same level, the only distinction being the manner in which they respond to the needs of others, in laying aside their dignity and status to be of help.—1971

APRIL 2

John 19:18. *There they crucified him, and with him two others, one on either side, with Jesus between them.*

God is speaking to you and me through the cross of Christ, showing us what we are like.

Have I ever had in my heart any of the pride of position that was in the hearts of the high priests? Have I ever washed my hands of some responsibility, as did Pilate? Have I partaken of the brutality of the Roman soldiers by taking part in a cruel conversation? Have I been a little dishonest like the politicians or fickle like the mob? Have I injured an innocent person either directly or indirectly? Or have I ever stood by while others were being hurt physically or slandered—and done nothing?

Let us not miss the meaning of this passage by blaming it on ancient figures and failing to see that it is our human nature that stands at the foot of the cross.—1944

APRIL 3

Matthew 27:59-60. *So Joseph took the body and wrapped it in a clean linen cloth and laid it in his own new tomb, which he had hewn in the rock. He then rolled a great stone to the door of the tomb and went away.*

A young missionary in India lay dying in extreme pain, the result of an accident. He seemed to be past speech, but his lips moved. One of his friends, kneeling beside him, caught the words, "And we indeed justly" (Luke 23:41, KJV).

The words of the dying thief! Could we take them on our lips, if we were called to such suffering today?

This passage of scripture calls us to quiet self-examination. "Were you there when they crucified my Lord? Were you there?" He lies there very quietly on the rocky shelf. He makes no passionate appeal to us. Let us kneel there beside him, and think what it all means. He had to die that we might live. If we are to live through him, we must die also to self and to sin.

"And we indeed justly."

"Were you there when they laid him in the tomb? Were you there?"—1938

APRIL 4

1 Corinthians 15:20-23. *Christ has been raised from the dead, the first fruits of those who have died. For since death came through a human being, the resurrection of the dead has also come through a human being; for as all die in Adam, so all will be made alive in Christ. But each in his own order: Christ the first fruits, then at his coming those who belong to Christ.*

Is Jesus alive today? This question is much more vital than "Did he survive the cross?" The answer to this question brings the Easter triumph into the present moment!

How did the disciples know Jesus to be alive on the first Easter Day? Some saw him with their own eyes and recognized him. Some met those who had seen him and believed their words. Others did not have the conviction that he was actually alive until he "showed himself" to them.

Is Jesus alive today? You can answer it for yourself and say with Saint Paul, "It is no longer I who live, but it is Christ who lives in me" (Galatians 2:20).—1943

APRIL 5

Matthew 28:10. *Then Jesus said to them, "Do not be afraid."*

I once conducted a service of worship shortly after Easter for the patients of a mental hospital. I began by asking the congregation, mostly patients, what they thought the first words spoken by Jesus when he returned to the disciples might have been. They answered, "Do not be afraid."

Those who are ill in the way that those patients were know with a certain instinct what the words of life are. When the struggle for existence has defeated you, you withdraw into fear: fear of enemies in the far distance; fear of "them"; even fear of yourself. Life is lived in terms of suspicion, never of trust.

We all exist on a continuum, I think, with those patients; we are all somewhat ill. Jesus comes and wipes away our fear. For many of us it is the fear of being wrong, the fear that we will be less than we thought we were, the fear that we will fail and our dreams come to nothing. If we will hear his words and trust him, then we can start again, this time on the basis of a sure hope, never again because we are afraid.—1987

APRIL 6

Matthew 21:22. *Whatever you ask for in prayer with faith, you will receive.*

Anyone who prays has surely had the experience of a seemingly unanswered prayer. How can this be, when the scriptures tell us we will receive that for which we ask in prayer? Among vexing theological problems, this one is near the top of the list.

I don't pretend to have it all figured out, and I am suspicious of people who have quick answers to this and other theological puzzles. As I try to understand what the scriptures say and reconcile it to my own experience and the stories of others, I think we have to back up and look at the big picture.

Jesus teaches us that when we pray "with faith" or, elsewhere, "for the kingdom," we will receive these things. In other words, our prayers need to be in alignment with God's purposes for us and our world. Most of my own prayers are for wisdom, for understanding, for change in my own heart. I'm not sure that's the right approach, but it is where my journey has taken me for now. Perhaps we Christians would do well to pray together more often, not just on Sundays but throughout the week. Praying together might help us pray in faith, for the kingdom.—2013

APRIL 7

Luke 24:30-31. *He took bread, blessed and broke it, and gave it to them. Then their eyes were opened, and they recognized him.*

Rembrandt etched this scene of recognition. A kind of bright unbroken light pours from the face of Christ as the two disciples know him "in the breaking of the bread." Do you discern the Lord in the breaking of the bread? If not, what is wrong?

In the words of institution at the Last Supper, Jesus set forth the entire meaning of his life's work in speaking of the "new covenant in my blood" (Luke 22:20). The bread and wine represent in a visible and physically partaken way the new life he opened up for us by virtue of the Atonement. When you "take" communion, you grasp onto the greatest possibility in the world: forgiveness, peace, and hope in the now.

If your communion is pallid, or mystifying, or dead in the effect, it is because the meaning behind it has lost contact with your need. You need a more vital explanation of it, or a more penetrating glimpse into your own gaps. When you are given both of these things, the communion will "send" you, and your eyes will be opened again, and you will recognize the Lord in the midst of your life.—1993

APRIL 8

Luke 24:41. *In their joy they were disbelieving and still wondering.*

As the disciples stood dumbfounded, Jesus did not deliver a theological discourse. Instead, he asked them a very human question, "Have you anything to eat?" How typical of Jesus this was! He was still their friend, sharing their life with them. He had always been like that, sharing the simple joys and problems of fishermen, living by a code of love that was simplicity itself, forgiving and healing without elaborate formulas, but with a simple "Go, and sin no more," or "Arise; you are whole."

That simple meal of broiled fish is a symbol of the simplicity of the Lord's Supper. The risen Lord is always present with his followers in the simple meal he has given us. He promises also to be with us when-ever we think of him or talk of him or read of him. The symbolic evidence of that truth is his explanation to the disciples of the fulfillment of Old Testament prophecy. He spoke just after eating. These are the two simple and loving ways in which he has been present with his disciples down through the ages: in the Sacrament, the simple holy meal; and in the Word, the simple holy story of God's love.—1969

☙❧

APRIL 9

John 21:12-14. *Jesus said to them, "Come and have breakfast." Now none of the disciples dared to ask him. "Who are you?" because they knew it was the Lord. Jesus came and took the bread and gave it to them, and did the same with the fish. This was now the third time that Jesus appeared to the disciples after he was raised from the dead.*

The scene shifts to Galilee, but the apostles are still mystified. Had they not a right to be? Could mortal men be expected to adjust themselves in a few days to such a world-shaking fact as Jesus' resurrection?

No matter how much he used earthly and everyday assurances, the Lord in his risen body must have had marvelous properties whose glory neither they nor we could grasp. But here is a point that ought to be of great comfort. Even in his mysterious, glorified risen state, the Lord is just as mindful as ever he was in the old days of the earthly needs of his people. "Children, you have no fish, have you?"

What can this mean to a believer in his pain, his deficiency, unemployment, or whatever distress? We can lift up our hearts to one who knows, who cares, and who will supply our need—or make us able to bear it.—1950

APRIL 10

Mark 16:15. *And he said to them, "Go into all the world and proclaim the good news to the whole creation."*

In the most ancient manuscripts of the Gospel of Mark the story breaks off abruptly after "they were afraid." Later copies added the verses we have just read. In still other manuscripts, after verse 8, the scribe has added: But they reported briefly to Peter and to those who were with him all that they had been told, and after this Jesus sent out by means of them, from east to west, "the sacred and imperishable proclamation of eternal salvation."

Although the original conclusion may be unknown, the Bible tells us as briefly as can be stated what happened after Easter: the disciples were sent to proclaim the gospel to the world.

The first response to the news of Christ's resurrection was not joy but fear, and there is always about it something truly awe-inspiring. For Easter means not only that Jesus lives, but that he is the Lord who shall come again with glory to judge both the living and the dead. As people who must stand before the judgment seat of Christ, we are to live all our days not only in God's love but also in that reverent fear of the Lord which Proverbs 9:10 calls "the beginning of wisdom."—1951

APRIL 11

John 20:19-20. *Jesus came and stood among them and said, "Peace be with you." After he said this, he showed them his hands and his side. Then the disciples rejoiced when they saw the Lord.*

After driving a motor car all day, you are tired partly because so many pictures, so many things, come before you in a very short time. In twelve hours you see miles and miles of countryside, cities, people, gas stations, other cars. Then at night you arrive home and you are at peace. If you know when to stop, you don't get tired out. And you are ready to go on again tomorrow.

In the abundant life which Jesus promises, we have to stop from time to time. There is the daily grind of things to be done, people to be seen, and we want to do our best. We can go forward more effectively if we stop at intervals to refuel and rest. Progress in the path of Christ requires moments of recollection, when you sit still (or kneel) to study the map. You don't want to make a lot of unnecessary detours. Rest yourself in Christ's peace, and let him send you on again. He knows the right route.

Pray that into your congregation or group the risen Christ may come with his peace, that these disciples may see the Lord and be glad.—1936

❧❧❧

APRIL 12

Luke 22:19. *Then he took a loaf of bread, and when he had given thanks, he broke it and gave it to them, saying, "This is my body, which is given for you. Do this in remembrance of me."*

When the priest invites the congregation to join her around the altar, and I rush to the back of the chapel to repeat the invitation aloud, in English and Spanish, "Everyone is invited to the table. Everyone!"

We are all welcome—the homeless man sitting in the back row, those with canes, walkers, and wheelchairs, the shy Latino unmarried couple who came with a four-week-old baby in their arms. When we say everyone, we really mean it. We join the prayers of the sick and the lonely, and the circle expands. We join the prayers of refugees desperately trying to reach Athens, Sweden, or Toronto, and the circle expands.

We join your prayers as well. In fact we join the prayers of every person who prays. We hold hands, say the Lord's Prayer, and share the bread and the wine. We are not just taking in the body of Christ—we are becoming the Body of Christ.—2016

APRIL 13

John 14:23. *Jesus answered him, "Those who love me will keep my word, and my Father will love them, and we will come to them and make our home with them."*

Today we consider Jesus' answer to another of the disciples' questions: "Lord, how is it that you will reveal yourself to us, and not to the world?" (John 14:22).

Does our God withhold himself? Jesus' response to the question definitely implies access by all people to God's love, but it also implies that not all will claim that love. In other words, anyone in "the world" may indeed know Christ manifest, if that one loves Christ and keeps Christ's word. But then the question must be asked, could anyone so transformed in affection and action be described as "in the world?"

Perhaps the transforming quality of love is at the heart of things here (as everywhere else). People motivated by affection and deep loyalties are known to be capable of magnanimous actions. They seem to find more joy in the doing of these than do those who simply comply with regulations.

Jesus is describing cause and effect. If one enters this loving union with him, it is the nature of things that the desire to keep to this specific way of living will grow. Forever.—1981

❧❧❧❧

APRIL 14

John 15:10. *I have kept my Father's commandments and abide in his love.*

Because we are spiritually short-sighted, we often miss the incarnations of God in the commonplace events and people about us. We miss the glory that shines out of pain, the patience that illumines discouragement, the courage that radiates from failure, the faith that makes the faces of ordinary folk glow.

In order to welcome God in the work she was doing about the house, a woman composed the following meditation:

"When opening the door, I pray thee, Lord, to open the door of my heart that I may receive thee, Lord, within. When washing clothes, I pray thee, Lord, to wash my heart, and make it pure as snow. When sweeping the floor, I pray thee, Lord, to sweep my heart from all evil, and make it clean. When receiving or sending a letter, I pray thee, Lord, to give me more faith that I may hold more constant communication with thee. When lighting the lamp, I pray thee, Lord, to let thy true light shine within my heart, and make me in all that I do to be kind and good like a lamp which lightens others."—1955

APRIL 15

John 15:19. *If you belonged to the world, the world would love you as its own. Because you do not belong to the world, but I have chosen you out of the world— therefore the world hates you.*

Christ calls his disciples to the service of God, not of the world. The two forms of service are incompatible. Saint James says bluntly: "Friendship with the world is enmity with God" (James 4:4).

Many professing Christians, hoping to avoid conflict between the two, attempt an uneasy compromise. Jesus warns sternly against such folly: "You cannot serve God and wealth" (Matthew 6:24). In these critical days, a compromising Christian is a very poor representative of the Lord Jesus Christ.

The world has been defined as "society organized apart from the will of God." It is a tremendously powerful society. Its lure is universal, its rewards enticing, its tyranny diabolical. Those who steadfastly hold to God's will and way, as revealed in Jesus, invite the hatred of the world. Jesus himself experienced the full fury of this hatred. He serves strong notice that those who follow him must expect similar treatment.

A person who is loyal to Jesus is prepared to die daily for him. But, said Thomas à Kempis sadly: "All desire to rejoice with Jesus; few are willing to endure anything for him, or with him."—1955

APRIL 16

John 16:12. *I still have many things to say to you, but you cannot bear them now.*

We are doomed to hopeless frustration if we assume, as many Christians have, that the only way we can learn the Lord's will in our concrete decisions and dilemmas is to "look it up in the Bible." The Bible is not a book of prescriptive oracles. As an old hymn tells us, "New occasions teach new duties." New eras in human life bring new problems. We are, literally, always in a new situation. What does the Lord want us to do in it?

Christ told us before his death that he had many things more to tell us and teach us. He promised that he would go on teaching us, showing us his will for us down through the ages, through his blessed Spirit who dwells in us, who takes the things of Christ and shows them to us. And he keeps that promise with all who keep faith with him and rely upon him. In every new situation we shall have his light to guide us, if we turn to him in meditation, prayer, obedience; if we "practice the presence." We don't find all the answers in the Bible; but in the light of the ever-present Christ we see light.—1970

APRIL 17

John 16:33. *In the world you face persecution. But take courage; I have conquered the world!*

Be assured of one thing: life has a goal. The story of your life, like a novel, has a plot. There are times when it seems true that "life is one darn thing after another." Or, as the Gospel of John says, "In the world you face persecution." Experience teaches us that Murphy's Law is quite correct, "If anything can go wrong—it will."

There are two orders of time, and we live in both at the same time. One is circular, cyclical. Things recur. Progress is absent.

But time also moves in a straight line from a beginning, through a midpoint and to an end, a logical and fulfilled conclusion. At that end everything comes together. God's will is done.

Therefore, we are pleased to know that in the love and power of Christ, the ultimate reality is: "But take courage; I have conquered the world." Life has a goal and a direction, as it has been created and redeemed by God in Christ. No matter what happens now—and it will—we are going somewhere. And the somewhere is new life in Christ. Easter is neither a blip nor an aberration. Easter is what life is really all about.—1996

APRIL 18

John 21:19. *After this he said to him, "Follow me."*

"Follow me" may be thought of as a duty or an invitation, but we will never achieve a life worthy of the name Christian if we neglect to think of it at all. This gospel has been called a "gospel of love" because Jesus was love in action, or in the familiar phrase, "he went about doing good." So too must all who are of his company. He did not spend his time searching out saints to do his work: he took simple, ordinary people who responded to the command "Follow me," and as they did the work, grateful people came to call them saints.

The difficulty many people find in the Christian faith is that it does make demands, and not trivial demands, either. It is not an abstract theological doctrine which can be satisfied by a recitation of the creeds: always we hear the voice of Jesus saying, "Follow me." Many find it an easy thing to recite "I believe in God;" no one will find it an easy matter to follow Christ, yet that is both our duty and our great reward.—1957

APRIL 19

Mark 2:16. *Why does he eat with tax collectors and sinners?*

One of the things I am most sure about in this life is that Jesus loves sinners. He loves us in the midst of our brokenness and determination to be difficult on general principle. And he doesn't just love the hope of the resurrected version of us. He loves us in the very present moment of our sin, in our reluctance to be vulnerable to our Creator.

We don't get to hide disarray from Jesus. Jesus sees our sin, our hurt, our shame, and refuses to compare, quantify, or qualify it. There is no ranking order of sin. Jesus simply knows it is there, wants to take it away, repair the breach, raise what was dead to new life. He sits with each of us—taxers of emotion and prostitutes of productivity, murderers of hope and addicts of power.

Instead of being ashamed of us, Jesus calls us his friends and keeps coming to find us, no matter where we are or what names people call us. Jesus loves us. And this passage of Mark challenges me to think that Jesus might love the biggest messes among us the very most. Jesus realizes that lifting us up, helping us hold his love in our lives, is a labor of such magnitude that he would die and rise again to help us learn it.—2015

APRIL 20

Matthew 3:7. *You brood of vipers!*

Before we can have Christ, we must hear and heed John the Baptist. What the world needs now is a voice crying in the moral wilderness, a voice that will be heard, a voice which, like John's, will convince people that they really need a Savior.

Here lies the basic reason for the fact that after two millennia of Christian history, the world and its people have remained pretty much the same—unaffected, unchanged. Before you want a Savior, you must be convinced that you are a sinner in need of saving. You must come to the devastating point of crying out: "Save me, Lord; I can't do it by myself!"

It is a pitiful paradox that we live in a sin-saturated society with little consciousness of sin. Psychiatrist Karl Menninger was moved to write a book called *Whatever Became of Sin*? Modern people do not like to use the word. We prefer to speak instead of social maladjustment, neurosis, peer pressure—but never sin.

John the Baptist, where are you now that we need you?—1980

APRIL 21

Psalm 38:17. *Truly, I am on the verge of falling, and my pain is always with me.*

It is not uncommon for us to edit our prayers. That usually happens when we are feeling inadequate, when we have violated God's expectations of us in some conspicuous way. Having sinned, we are too ashamed to bring before God the anguish and shame we feel. We suspect that the very admission of our guilt will be an offense to the divine sensibilities.

Of course that is absurd. God knows. God knows our every frailty, our every fault. To read the Psalms is to be reminded, over and over, of God's steady willingness to hear us out, to hear our shame and our regret as much as to hear of our triumphs and our joys. "O Lord, you know all my desires, and my sighing is not hidden from you," says the author of Psalm 38. That psalmist also describes a life that "by reason of my foolishness" is "utterly bowed down and prostrate." The psalmist flings the story of his life upon the divine mercy, knowing that God knows everything, believing that God accepts and affirms even as God knows all that can be known.

This is a great encouragement to us. God invites our every prayer, our every anguish, our every fear, our every shame. God invites all of that, refusing to forsake us.—1955

APRIL 22

Matthew 4:1-3. *Then Jesus was led up by the Spirit into the wilderness to be tempted by the devil. He fasted forty days and forty nights, and afterwards he was famished. The tempter came and said to him, "If you are the Son of God, command these stones to become loaves of bread."*

The temptation story puzzles us, partly because it is told in pictorial language and partly because it seems so different from the sort of temptations that beset us.

Perhaps we can never expect to understand all that went on in our Lord's mind and soul during those days. But there is one word which helps us understand—the little word "if." "If you are the Son of God." That was the doubt that tormented him. How could he be sure that the Father had chosen him? Wasn't there some way to prove that he was right?

To a lesser degree we are tormented by the same doubt. How can we be sure that God is real or that Christ is right? Must we live by faith and not by sight? Jesus defeated the devil in the desert, but Satan returned, often, to the attack. While Jesus hung on the cross, the chief priest repeated the tempter's phrase, "If you are the Son of God..."—1949

APRIL 23

Colossians 2:19. *...holding fast to the head, from whom the whole body, nourished and held together by its ligaments and sinews, grows with a growth that is from God.*

Paul is using one of his favorite metaphors, comparing the body of Christ, the church, to a human body. You might compare yourself, as a living member of Christ's body, to a little toe, or, if you are humbler in your self-estimate, to a single tiny cell. Rudolf Virchow, the great pioneer pathologist, defined the human body as "a cell state in which every cell is a citizen." Every cell of Christ's body is a human being of infinite importance—and value—to Christ.

In any body, the mutual interdependence of the cells is such that each cell is important for the body to grow and flourish.

When the church—even a small part of it—is growing in Christ-likeness, it is experiencing the only growth that is from God. Other increases may develop from this, such as growth in numbers, in assets, in influence for good. But the only growth that comes surely from God is growth of the members in the likeness of God's Son, our Lord. Dietrich Bonhoeffer spoke the whole truth in these words: "What matters in the church is not religion but the form of Christ, and its taking form amidst a band of men."—1989

APRIL 24

Matthew 4:23. *Jesus went throughout Galilee, teaching in their synagogues and proclaiming the good news of the kingdom and curing every disease and every sickness among the people.*

Our Lord's ministry, from the beginning to the end, consisted of these three activities: teaching the truth of God; preaching the love of God; and healing sick bodies and souls by the power of God.

If, as we believe, the ministry of the church is the ministry of Christ, carried on through the faithful, it follows that the Christian ministry—Jesus' ministry—must continue to be this three-fold ministry of teaching, preaching, and healing. Our Lord's ministry in his incarnate life is the standard by which we are to judge the church's ministry.

Every ordained person and every layperson should be aware of this at all times. To serve Christ is to teach God's truth, to preach God's love, and to heal the sick by God's power. Anything else we do is secondary to that, or a false substitute for the ministry of the Lord himself to which he has called us.—1959

APRIL 25

Revelation 7:16-17. *They will hunger no more, and thirst no more; the sun will not strike them, nor any scorching heat; for the Lamb at the center of the throne will be their shepherd, and he will guide them to springs of the water of life, and God will wipe away every tear from their eyes.*

We are all members of two families.

We belong to our earthly family. Even in the most wonderful earthly family we encounter brokenness, grief, hurt, and regret. Because of free will, illness, speech without thought, sin and death, we suffer. This is the price we pay for being human, and even with the grace of God we cannot avoid some of these experiences.

But if we are Christians, then we have another family in which we are all the children of God. There is no brokenness, sin, unforgiveness, or pain. Within God's loving arms there is no death. Jesus, our shepherd, leads us to springs of living water—and God wipes away all tears from our eyes. In this family of God, there is a perfection which comes only by being in his presence.—1976

APRIL 26

Mark 16:15. *Go into all the world and proclaim the good news to the whole creation.*

When Forward Movement began in 1935 it was not a publishing house but a renewal movement in the Episcopal Church, established by General Convention to counter the spiritual malaise of the Depression. Volunteers went from diocese to diocese, calling on people to commit themselves afresh to the basic principles of discipleship. They organized conferences and workshops on mission, on Bible study, and on the leadership of prayer groups. It was a great success. Enthusiasm developed rapidly, and the morale of the church was much improved. The publishing program grew from this, as a means to provide resources for evangelism, education, and spiritual growth.

When the gospel was first preached by the disciples it, too, was a movement of the spirit, depending on the testimony of eyewitnesses and people's memory of what Jesus taught, passed on by word of mouth. Mark was one of the first to see the need for writing things down in a permanent and organized form, so people everywhere might know the basic facts about Jesus and what he said and did. His brief account is still the best starting point for new Christians. Give thanks for Mark and Paul, the first Christian authors.—1991

❦❧❦❧

APRIL 27

Matthew 5:14. *You are the light of the world.*

It was two weeks after Christmas, and my little grandson and I were taking down my Christmas tree. We had put the ornaments into their boxes, and I was removing the strings of lights. One string lay on the floor.

Thad picked it up and plugged one end into the other. He looked at it in a puzzled way, and asked, "Hot? Hot?"

No, Thad, the bulbs will not light up and get hot. The beautiful colored lights will not shine and sparkle unless the light string is plugged into the electric power outlet.

I spend a lot of time being plugged into myself. As long as I'm stewing and fretting, thinking that I need to control my little world and the people in it, as long as I try to do things on my own power, I'm like the string of colored lights, plugged into itself.

It's only when I turn things over to God's care that I can be a light in the world.—1993

APRIL 28

Matthew 5:17. *Do not think that I have come to abolish the law or the prophets; I have come not to abolish but to fulfill.*

There is something intimidating about Jesus and the demands that he makes in the Sermon on the Mount. I sometimes want to say, "Jesus, please leave me alone, let go of your impossible expectations, and let me live my life in peace! You ask too much." Thank heaven, though, that Jesus knows me better than I know myself, that he sees buried deep down within me the seeds of a loving way of life, seeds I no longer see.

Life has hardened me, as it probably has you, and I tend to become cynical about such teachings as "Turn the other cheek." But in Jesus it becomes clear that people can forgive, share, be reconciled, and make peace; such a way of life is not an empty dream or idle fantasizing. It is possible both because God created us to live in such a way, and because Jesus activates, so to speak, the latent potential.

Many people in the course of my life have brought out the best in me in some way; but only one has used unconditional love as the means to that end, because only one has that love.—1987

APRIL 29

1 Thessalonians 2:19-20. *For what is our hope or joy or crown of boasting before our Lord Jesus at his coming? Is it not you? Yes, you are our glory and joy!*

Paul is so often cranky that it is easy to forget how much he loves the people he served. The Thessalonians were particularly dear to his heart, and he told them so. When he presented the fruits of his labor to the Lord Jesus, Paul did not produce a list of the miles he had traveled or the jail terms he had served, but of people like the Thessalonians, who were Paul's glory and joy, the crown of his boasting. These grace-filled verses remind us that we do not always grieve the heart of God. Yes, we have fresh sins to confess each week, and yes, we fall short in our imitation of Christ. But we also manage to participate in moments of generosity, forgiveness, and genuine love that surprise even us. This raises the possibility that we too might bring some hope and joy to God's heart, as we grow in our understanding of what it means to be faithful.

If you have never tried it, spend one minute today—just sixty seconds—letting God love you. While you sit there quietly, listen to your mind tell you all the reasons why you are not worthy. Then tell it to hush. You are God's glory and joy. You are God's beloved child. —1999

✿✿✿

APRIL 30

Matthew 5:37. *Let your word be "Yes, Yes" or "No, No"; anything more than this comes from the evil one.*

If people are going to lie, they're going to lie, no matter how fervently they swear on a stack of Bibles that they will tell nothing but the truth. It is better, then, to have done with the whole business of swearing on stacks of Bibles and everything like it.

Let our words be true and let them be few. This is what our Lord is saying.

We of the modern West are not so much given to elaborate oath-taking as were the ancient Easterners, but we are still tempted, as all people are, to use words to conceal what we mean rather than to say what we mean. Somebody dies, and we say that he "passed away." Instead of saying, "When I die," we say, "If anything happens to me." Somebody sins, and we say that she "made a mistake." Such words are deceitful. Their purpose is to conceal some unwelcome truth. And we all know people who will not be frank and open with us, but pour forth torrents of palaver. How easily we can do it, too, saying that we only want to be polite.

"Let your word be 'Yes, Yes' or 'No, No,'" says our Lord.—1959

MAY

MAY 1

2 Corinthians 4:4. *In their case the god of this world has blinded the minds of the unbelievers, to keep them from seeing the light of the gospel of the glory of Christ, who is the image of God.*

"World" has meant many things to Christians over the centuries, but there is always one basic thing: the world is the society or culture in which one lives, and more particularly the aspects of it that are at war with Christ.

Always there is the temptation to conform to the world, and out of this conformity come tensions. Even though much of it calls itself Christian, the world we live in is a pretty hard place in which to be a Christian.

When our Lord says: "Therefore I tell you, do not worry about your life, what you will eat, or about your body, what you will wear" (Luke 12:22), the world says: "You need security against poverty, sickness, and old age. Today doesn't matter; only the future counts." Instead of "Love your enemies, do good to those who hate you" (Luke 6:27), the world says: "Hate your enemies. Be ready to strike before they strike you. Contain them; don't trust them." Instead of "For one's life does not consist in the abundance of possessions" (Luke 12:15), the world says: "Earn more. Spend more. Be comfortable. Live it up. Enjoy life."—1962

MAY 2

Acts 11:9. *What God has made clean, you must not call profane.*

There is something in us which believes that when something is so once, it is always so. An applicant for a job as rector wrote that he had spent some time in prison, had been asked to leave towns on several occasions, and had often been in court. Of course his application was turned down. The amazed vestry was then told that the application could easily have been from Saint Paul, whose resume would have included all those things.

The prejudicial outlook "Once a jailbird, always a jailbird" would deny to the church the benefits of a Paul and his gifts for evangelism.

The early church was in a dilemma. They wanted to remain true to their Judaic past but they also had to acknowledge that God was calling those into his fold who were not of Jewish background. What to do? At first Peter and Paul took opposite positions, Peter seeking to limit church membership to Jews and Paul wanting to welcome everyone. Paul's vision of a church with arms wide open prevailed. We are called to be loyal to old traditions even as we act in new ways. That calls for us to accept a lot of inconsistency. We need God's grace in order to do so.—1990

MAY 3

Psalm 57:1. *In the shadow of your wings will I take refuge.*

No one in the climbing party saw the storm coming. From the eastern face of the mountain there was no way of knowing that a major storm was approaching from the west. The minute they realized the weather was going to turn, they ceased their ascent and tried to return to the base camp. It was too late. They had to find shelter on the mountain. They were fortunate to find a formation in the rock face that served as a small cave. The climbers huddled together and soon realized how blessed they were to have found such a place, for the storm contained winds that would have blown them off the mountain. Minutes earlier they had been cursing the rocky face of the mountain for being so tough and unforgiving. Now those very characteristics were keeping them alive.

This story brings to life the imagery of the psalmist.Both the story and the psalm tell of God as a refuge. God provides the haven we need when the winds of life become fierce and dangerous.—2000

MAY 4

Leviticus 16:31. *It is a sabbath of complete rest to you, and you shall deny yourselves.*

And what shall we deny ourselves? In the Sunday paper an article described a rural farmer who lives on a total annual income of about $2,000. He grows most of his own food, makes and repairs his own clothing and tools, and has neither electricity nor plumbing in his farmhouse. The comments of amazement I've heard are not so much about how this man lives on such a small amount of money, but about how delighted he is with his life.

Through self-denial the farmer is living a Sabbath life—not a life of deprivation and hardship, but a life of zest, of enthusiastic appreciation for the beauty around him. He works hard, and he rests, and he enjoys the view! He knows the meaning of complete rest. Do you?

What is your understanding of Sabbath? What would you change in order to allow yourself to rest completely? What would you deny yourself?

The rabbis know that God has gifts for us that we can only receive within the Sabbath. Only then is there room in our hearts to receive. There is quiet there, so God can speak and be heard.—2000

MAY 5

Leviticus 19:9. *You shall not reap to the very edges of your field.*

The command against reaping the corners of the field goes back to the primitive belief in spirits who had authority over the land. A place to dwell and food to eat had to be left for them or they would leave the farmer. Now Israel has given the old law a new humanitarian bent: We are not to take everything for ourselves but to leave something for the one less fortunate than we.

To plow the field up to the last furrow, to attempt to scrape the last bit of profit from one's labor, betokens a miserly spirit which in the end works to its own disadvantage. Agricultural science is now awakening to this ecological truth. To drain the potholes and the marshlands, to plow up the submarginal lands, is to create floods and dust bowls.

We need this "concern for the corner" operative in the city as well as the country, and not the contractor who uses the cheapest possible material, replacing one slum with another soon-to-be, or the housing developer who crowds in as many apartments as possible in his highrise. Without concern for the corner we will poison our streams, kill the lakes, pollute the air, and destroy the quality of human living.—1971

MAY 6

Matthew 6:33. *Strive first for the kingdom of God and his righteousness, and all these things will be given to you as well.*

This is the thing that makes people shake their heads. Of all periods of human history, ours is the one when science and reason have unlocked so many secrets of nature that production has increased many times over.

And yet we cannot allay the specter of war nor save millions from starvation. Intellect alone cannot bring about a better world.

It is because we have not put first things first. We have not first sought the kingdom of God and his righteousness. We have first sought our own profit and our own security and have wanted God to back us up to these ends.

We wanted financial return above everything else. We got it, and now we cannot buy with it what we would like to buy. Slowly, painfully, we are beginning to realize that security for any one of us lies in greater abundance for all of us. "Seek ye first the kingdom."
—1947

MAY 7

Matthew 7:12. *In everything do to others as you would have them do to you.*

Someone has drawn a caricature of the medieval lord speaking to his subjects from the castle balcony: "Remember the Golden Rule," he is saying, "whoever has the gold makes the rules!"

Too often that seems to be true. "Money talks," we say, or "If you've got enough money you can get away with anything." Seldom do the acquisition of money and a high ethical standard go together. Proof is all around us: the poor of the world, battered and polluted nations, war-torn countries, men and women run over by the juggernaut of greed in one way or another. Those blessed with wealth—individuals or nations—will someday stand at the judgment seat. Those who have the gold will be called on to justify the rules they made and explain the ones they broke. Money is power, and the Bible shouts the warning that God will hold responsible those to whom he gives power.

The Golden Rule has nothing to do with rules. It has to do with love. Whoever has the gold must give it away.—1973

MAY 8

Matthew 7:13-14. *Enter through the narrow gate; for the gate is wide and the road is easy that leads to destruction, and there are many who take it. For the gate is narrow and the road is hard that leads to life, and there are few who find it.*

We drivers all know a danger spot where the right road is a quick, narrow turn just where the wrong road stretches ahead broad and inviting. After we have gone down that easy wrong road a couple of times, we are on guard against it.

The road of penitence is like that. A companion's influence can draw us back into the old sin. Or in a company of associates, our resistance melts and we find ourselves joining in the very offenses we deplore.

The thing to do is to part company. This is not weakness; it is the avoidance of a known weakness. Nor need it be pride or lack of charity. We can remain humble and charitable while telling ourselves, "For my soul's sake, I must keep away."

The same is true of certain habits, certain situations, certain books. Do not toy with danger. Let us fill our time with something nobler which leaves no room for the temptation to enter.—1940

MAY 9

Acts 16:9. *Come over to Macedonia and help us.*

How many members of our mainline churches would understand you if you spoke of the Macedonian cry? Not many, I'm afraid. But our parents, possibly, and our grandparents, almost certainly, would instantly have recognized its meaning. The phrase was a watchword of missionary-minded Christians of an earlier day. They felt that the "man of Macedonia" was everywhere in the world of the unevangelized, praying for Christians to "come over and help us." If these mainline churches are languishing today, one reason for their decline is the loss of the missionary imperative. How long has it been since you have heard the hymn "From Greenland's Icy Mountains" sung in church?

Somehow we must recover our sense and awareness of the marching orders we have received from our Lord—to go into the world and preach the gospel to every living creature, baptizing them into Christ with water and in the Spirit. William Temple rightly said that the church exists primarily for the sake of those outside itself. —1983

MAY 10

Matthew 13:10-11. *Then the disciples came and asked him, "Why do you speak to them in parables?" He answered, "To you it has been given to know the secrets of the kingdom of heaven..."*

What is the kingdom? It is what we must have—you and I, everyone. Jesus came to be the kingdom, to bring it, to open it to everyone. We cannot know its entirety but we can live in it. Jesus was too wise to offer us a photograph of the kingdom. Instead, he kept saying, "It is like this, it is like that." As his hearers got his meaning, so we can get it if we want to.

We know what we mean when we say "the animal kingdom" or "the vegetable kingdom." It is the way these living things grow and live together. It is their world. Something surrounds them—we call it law, but it is more than that. They never break out of its bounds. It is their life.

Do we have anything like that? We belong to the animal kingdom, but we can't stay there. We keep breaking out. We yearn and grope for something else. There must be a different kingdom for human beings. Jesus gives the answer: The only place for you to be yourself is in the kingdom of God. Keep seeking it. I have opened the kingdom to you.—1938

MAY 11

Psalm 78:38. *But he was so merciful that he forgave their sins and did not destroy them.*

It's been months since I have heard any new rock songs. This spring I gave up my favorite radio station. It wasn't easy, but when I heard the disc jockeys laughing one day about living in the state that leads the nation in executing people and then saying they were proud to live in "the death machine state," I had to take a stand.

Last week, on another radio station, the hosts were talking about Oklahoma leading the nation in incarcerating women and were making jokes about them. I could overlook their ignorance until they said, "On a more serious note, on Wall Street, stock prices continue to fall." That was too much. Prices more important than people?

I suppose taking potshots at people in prison is easy. I too make jokes when I am uncomfortable or scared. If our prison problem doesn't scare you or make you uncomfortable, then you're not paying attention.

I know firsthand that we and the people in our prisons are children of the very same God. And I know God wants prisoners to receive compassion, forgiveness, and life, though they may not deserve it. I know it because that's how God has treated me.—2002

MAY 12

Psalm 68:19. *Blessed be the Lord day by day, the God of our salvation, who bears our burdens.*

Deep in the traditions of Christians, Jews, and Muslims is the understanding of the necessity of the daily praise of God.

Muslims have never seen prayer as "asking." They know little of petitions in prayer, yet every Muslim is required to praise God five times a day, at dawn, at noon, in late afternoon, at sunset, and at night.

Jews understand this, also. The tradition of Judaism is to pray three times a day (as Jesus and the disciples did) at morning, noon, and evening.

As author Herman Wouk says, "A man wants to praise God for the marvels of life, and to ask to be spared its terrors if possible, and to give thanks for what he has in hand, in health, family, and work. He wants to, that is, if a sense will not leave him that God is there."

Into this tradition, Christians enter and remain, praising God daily. Daily morning and evening prayer is the invitation of the church to all her children to join in the ceaseless and daily praise of God.—1968

MAY 13

Luke 24:50-53. *Then he led them out as far as Bethany, and, lifting up his hands, he blessed them. While he was blessing them, he withdrew from them and was carried up into heaven. And they worshiped him, and returned to Jerusalem with great joy; and they were continually in the temple blessing God.*

In an Italian church may be seen an unusual picture. At a glance, it is only another picture of the crucifixion. But as one looks, in the darkness of the church, the picture changes. Behind the figure of Christ rises a vast and shadowy figure. The nails that pierce the hands and the feet of Jesus go through to the hands and the feet of God. The spear thrust into his side goes through to God's.

Is not this the whole truth of Jesus' life? He was not just a fine man, who lived and died, but the man who revealed the true nature of all things—God in human life. His life and actions are the life and actions of God. His joys are God's joys; his suffering God's suffering; his love God's love. He is our Truth and our Way. He is the born, the living, the crucified, the resurrected, the ascended Lord.

So believe, and you will feel his hands outstretched and blessing you, and you will go on your way with great joy.—1942

MAY 14

Exodus 33:1. *The Lord said to Moses, "Go, leave this place, you and the people whom you have brought up out of the land of Egypt, and go to the land of which I swore to Abraham, Isaac, and Jacob."*

The Exodus story has always resonated with people who have been oppressed. African Americans celebrate it in gospel hymns and through the words of great preachers like Dr. Martin Luther King Jr. Peoples in Africa and the Caribbean have also found comfort in this story.

Today's passage from Exodus is set soon before the people finally enter the Promised Land. Much has happened since they left Egypt, and God is greatly disappointed. Moses must once more intercede, asking God to stay in their midst.

In America, the oprresion that Dr. King spoke about in his famous "I Have a Dream" speech in 1963 is still a reality for many who remain shackled by poverty, poor education, and joblessness. We need to do more than sing the words of freedom hymns. We must find a way to make the dream a reality and "march on till victory is won" (from *Lift Every Voice and Sing*)—2015

MAY 15

Matthew 9:11. *Why does your teacher eat with tax collectors and sinners?*

I was writing a poem and I wanted to use a synonym for God. I highlighted God and moved my cursor to the thesaurus icon at the top of the screen.

I clicked. God is not in the thesaurus, it said.

What? I chuckled at my computer's lack of God-consciousness and then began to get this mental image of God being everywhere, even in laptops. I've always thought God was in heaven and maybe in church. But he's also in here in prison, where murderers, thieves, rapists, child molesters, and drug dealers live. Among society's outcasts, that's where I found God. (Actually, it's where he found me. God wasn't lost. I was.)

It shouldn't be surprising that God could be in a prison. If Jesus were walking around today, what would people think about a son of God who spent most of his time in prisons, visiting the very people society had exiled? In crack houses? Shooting galleries? In parks with the homeless? Juvenile detentions? Mental institutions? Homes for unwed mothers? Slums?

To be Christ-like is to eat with sinners.

Have you seen Jesus lately?

Whom have you been eating with?

Pass the salt. Thank you.—1998

MAY 16

Acts 16:19. *But when her owners saw that their hope of making money was gone, they seized Paul and Silas and dragged them into the marketplace before the authorities.*

It was fine having Paul and Silas in town, preaching an interesting new religion—until they began to interfere with business. They healed this girl with the "spirit of divination" whose affliction was a money-maker for her masters. When religion starts meddling with something really important, such as the making of money, then it appears that religion is getting out of hand.

Is this crude and inhuman idea entirely dead? It is still possible to use human beings as mere sources of financial gain to their users. It is possible, and it is done by many people in many ways. When any child of God is used as productive property by others, the Christian religion must move in, in the Name of Christ, and put a halt to it. Either it does that or it is not the Christian religion.—1962

MAY 17

Ephesians 3:6. *The Gentiles have become fellow heirs, members of the same body, and sharers in the promise in Christ Jesus through the gospel.*

What dynamite this verse contained for the early church. For Judaism, the Gentile was the outsider. The Christian church, says Paul, is for everyone who needs it and wants it.

How is the church necessary as a way of making Christ known? Why can't we demonstrate the transforming power of Christ in human relations within our families, our communities, our nation? Because in the church Christ demonstrates the radical inclusiveness of his purpose. He wants all people to come into fellowship through him. A family is tied together by blood, a community by common responsibilities and interests, a nation by similar political outlooks and physical territory. What holds the church together? Only Christ. We open the doors of the church and anyone can come in who wants to—no entrance tests, no subscription fee, no claim to superior morality or spirituality. In just such a strange and motley group of people Christ proves his real power to create fellowship. That is why the church is his Body as no other society can be.—1959

MAY 18

Matthew 8:26. *Then he got up and rebuked the winds and the sea; and there was a dead calm.*

When I was called to be rector of a certain parish, I found a congregation split into factions, and parish life that could best be described as "a stormy sea." Several years later, as I left that parish, a very dear lady gave a stained glass window in thanksgiving for my ministry there. She chose as the theme of that beautiful window, "Christ Stilling the Storm."

How appropriate, for the calm that had come to that parish was Jesus' work, not mine. I had simply diverted their attention from their feuds and fusses and focused it on our Savior who says to all such storms, "Hush, be still!"

Those words can ring in any life which is opened to his voice. Lives that are torn apart with anxiety about tomorrow—rat-race lives worn out before their time, due to a frantic chasing after superficial values—and lives that are looking, terrified, into the face of death. All these can know the miracle of calm.

Just listen…and trust…that voice which says with such authority and such love, "Hush! Be still!" Do not wonder what sort of man is this that even the winds and the sea obey him.—1981

MAY 19

Ephesians 4:1-2. *I therefore, the prisoner in the Lord, beg you to lead a life worthy of the calling to which you have been called, with all humility and gentleness, with patience, bearing with one another in love.*

This passionate plea to the church is as pertinent today as when it was received in Ephesus. It makes the ultimate demand on each of us to lead a life worthy of our calling. What part does humility play in that life?

Humility, true humility, is the deep knowledge that God is to be sought, and found, and served in every person. Humility bows its heart to all, in acknowledgment of the presence of the Holy there. Humility can be silent in the vestry meeting, awaiting the truth that may emerge from another's perspective. Humility is the teacher who gladly learns from the student. Humility subverts pride and self-righteousness—especially when one is right.

The gift of humility comes from the heart of Jesus Christ to you. Jesus knows that humility will help you see others as he sees them, to hear in them his truth, and to learn from it. If we believe that every person, made in the image of God, bears some part of the truth the whole community needs, then humility before others can be the key to truth. Think of someone with whom you disagree on an important issue. Let the truth of this urgent passage work its way with you.
—2000

❧❧❧❧

MAY 20

Ephesians 4:32. *Be kind to one another, tenderhearted, forgiving one another.*

Christians are getting various kinds of labels these days. As people feel they are losing control, repression grows. There is less and less sympathy for those who are an embarrassment to us. And so those who still have compassion and understanding for the weak are labeled "bleeding hearts."

Christians are "bleeding hearts" because they are against the death penalty, try to rehabilitate drug abusers, want peace in the world, food for the hungry, and understanding for the alcoholic, the promiscuous, and the mentally ill. It should make us all feel better to realize that Jesus was a "bleeding heart." In the gospel for today he heals a paralytic. Saint Paul was also a "bleeding heart," and in our passage we see why. If your heart doesn't bleed for others, if you are not tenderhearted and forgiving and understanding, you cannot expect God to be tender with you. If you know how the Lord Christ bled for you, bleed for others. And wear the label "bleeding heart" with pride.—1971

MAY 21

Matthew 11:6. *And blessed is anyone who takes no offense at me.*

Offended by Jesus? Not I. Although I confess to being a timid evangelist. I recently invited a nonchurchgoing friend to a Bible study. Jane is intelligent and extremely well read, so I thought she would respond to the teacher's scholarly approach. She scowled: "I'm not interested in those old prophets, pointing their fingers and yelling 'God's gonna getcha!' "

Sigh. No worthy response came from these lips. If only I'd had the gumption, the quickness to say: But Jesus came to change all that. Read about him. Learn of his radical hospitality. Yes, God's going to "get you," in ways you've never imagined. As former Archbishop of Canterbury Rowan Williams says, "God will take your experiences, mistakes, and false starts and transform you so Christ's transfiguring love can show through." Jesus told John the Baptist: Look at what I do and you'll know who I am. I touch pain; soothe the restlessness of the human spirit. I am the giver of life.—2012

MAY 22

Ezekiel 36:26. *A new heart I will give you, and a new spirit I will put within you.*

One of the false assumptions operating in the world today, leaving wasted lives in its wake, is that if you can find the key, you can apply it to yourself and change yourself. Many people, captured by this assumption, wander from new thing to new thing, each promising to be the key that will bring some real change in character and behavior. One such person went through physical fitness, higher education, religion, sensitivity training, radical politics, and escapist novels. None of these effected any real change in his life. It is not true that a person can change himself.

Only God can change a person. Only God has the power to reach inside you and cleanse you of your guilt, heal you of the effects of others' sins, empower you to desire and obtain a whole new set of priorities and considerations, and behave consistently in an increasingly Christ-like manner. God is not reluctant to exercise this power, but he must be asked and believed, though not as thoroughly as one might think. God only needs the slimmest faith to move in and effortlessly to achieve the changes we have so arduously tried to accomplish.—1978

MAY 23

Acts 2:4. *All of them were filled with the Holy Spirit and began to speak in other languages, as the Spirit gave them ability.*

In Genesis, we read of the tower of Babel, a structure reaching to heaven built to acquire godlike powers. But the builders were confounded as people always are when they attempt equality with God. They could no longer understand each other's language, and the Lord scattered them over the face of the earth.

In contrast to the Babel chaos, on Pentecost the Holy Spirit swept into the room of believers and gave them the ability to speak and understand other languages. At Babel, people proved they could not build anything significant or lasting on their own terms, by their own power. On the Day of Pentecost, people were empowered by God to extend their community by preaching, healing, and baptizing in the name of Jesus, through the gifts of the Holy Spirit.

If Babel and its tower meant alienation, Pentecost and its power meant unity.

The gospel can be heard anywhere, in one's own language. The lonely hear an invitation. The sinful hear judgment. The guilty hear forgiveness. What will you hear today?—1982

MAY 24

Psalm 25:1. *To you, O Lord, I lift up my soul.*

I was the despair of my mathematics teacher at school. The whole business eluded me. Treated as backward and stupid by the schoolmaster, I feared and hated the subject and him.

Then one day a new teacher arrived who had a blessed and joyful qualification for all schoolboys: he was a cricketer of renown. We admired him for his athletic prowess. And for something else as well: he loved teaching as much as he loved cricket. I responded to his freshness of approach, his joy. I learned fast. Geometry and algebra opened their secrets to me. It was fun, because of him. Joy communicates itself, and the soul will learn from a joyful-hearted teacher. True it is that perfect love casts out fear, and the loving heart of the Lord injects its joy to the anxious, fearful believer, strengthening with forgiveness, with new hope, with fresh desire to love and serve, with confidence so that the soul shall dwell at ease. —1974

MAY 25

Matthew 12:33. *The tree is known by its fruit.*

We live in the world's richest country. So what is the United States doing about the worst homeless problem in its history? Shelters are so crammed they turn away record numbers of people—many of them children. Food pantries and soup kitchens are also overextended.

Twenty years ago, about a third of the homeless had mental problems, another third were addicted to alcohol or drugs, and only a third were thought to have the ability to develop skills for independent living.

Now it seems that more than half the folks seeking shelter are not only employable but employed, and still they have no place to live. In her book *Nickel and Dimed: On (Not) Getting By in America,* Barbara Ehrenreich tells of lower-rung wage earners having to live ten to a room to get by on their income.

For almost a generation, we have chosen largely to ignore the need for affordable housing and other programs for the needy. Political leaders are occupied with other matters. The crisis facing America's poor needs attention, and for now that attention is not likely to come from the government.

That leaves only us. Through prayer, each of us can discern a way to make someone else's life a little more sheltered. Shall we start today?—2005

MAY 26

Psalm 38:21-22. *O Lᴏʀᴅ, do not forsake me; be not far from me, O my God. Make haste to help me, O Lᴏʀᴅ of my salvation.*

Like the psalmist, we all at times feel isolated and lonely. Even our Lord felt it: "Could you not watch with me one hour?" he prayed at Gethsemane. Ours cannot be a loneliness like his, but we have all felt unwanted, that nobody cares. Many destitute, homeless, and forgotten people feel this today; and it is almost as bad to be alone in luxury.

The only hope, when we feel alone, is the realization that our Lord was alone, and that we, like him, may be relieved by the comfort of the everlasting arms of almighty God, "unto whom all hearts are open, all desires known, and from whom no secrets are hid."

Recall the words that George Bernard Shaw put into the mouth of Joan of Arc: "Do you think you can frighten me by telling me that I am alone? France is alone; and God is alone; and what is my loneliness before the loneliness of my country and my God?…Well, my loneliness shall be my strength too; it is better to be alone with God; His friendship will not fail me, nor His counsel, nor His love." —1939

❧❧❧❧

MAY 27

Psalm 37:7. *Be still before the LORD and wait patiently for him.*

Learning to be patient and to wait are lessons that do not come easily to many of us. But God waits for us: his time is infinite. Again and again, he gives us the chance to stop juggling the scattered pieces of our lives.

In our fast-paced, noisy world, how reassuring to be asked to be still and wait! Society encourages us to act quickly and to take charge, but God reminds us that he is in charge. What a relief it can be to give up the need to be in control all the time!

A friend described to me how, waiting in check-out lines or sitting in traffic, she became stressed, irritable, and generally unpleasant. When she began to acknowledge that these situations were beyond her control, she began to look on them as gifts. Now she welcomes these opportunities for contemplation and meditation. Prayer and silence have become vital parts of her day.

Because he loves us, God waits for us to seek his peace and serenity. We need only accept those gifts. (1994)

MAY 28

Matthew 13:33. *The kingdom of heaven is like yeast that a woman took and mixed in with three measures of flour until all of it was leavened.*

Many of Jesus' parables use images that are far from my experience. I've never found a great treasure or a wonderful pearl. I've never caught fish in a net. And where I live, mustard is a small plant that couldn't serve as a nesting place for even the smallest bird.

But this short parable is an image I know something about, although I'm sure that when Jesus said "yeast" it was something different from the little packets of granules in my refrigerator.

If you have never made anything with yeast, I encourage you to try it. Although it may be mysterious, it isn't difficult, and it can turn out to be a kind of meditation, as one mixes the yeast into the flour, adds the milk, sugar, salt, and oil, kneads it for a while until it is smooth, and then sets it in a warm place to rise.

The dough changes from a heavy, leaden lump into something light and airy. And the smell is wonderful.

The kingdom of heaven is like yeast. Not "pie in the sky," but bread in the oven. Light, beautiful, nourishing, warm. Let's enjoy it! —1993

MAY 29

1 Timothy 6:10. *The love of money is a root of all kinds of evil, and in their eagerness to be rich some have wandered away from the faith and pierced themselves with many pains.*

Listen to two comments by great American writers. Herman Melville wrote in Moby Dick: "The urbane activity with which a man receives money is really marvelous, considering that we so earnestly believe money to be the root of all earthly ills, and that on no account can a monied man enter heaven. Ah! How cheerfully we consign ourselves to perdition!"

Ralph Waldo Emerson wrote in his Journal: "Nothing can be more foolish than this reproach...of the love of dollars. It is like oxen taxing each other with eating grass, or a society of borers in an oak tree accusing one another of eating wood; or, in a great society of cheese-mites, if one should begin making insinuations that the other was eating cheese."

Both statements are wise. We really do want money and this is a healthy desire. The issue is whether we use money or money uses us. The love of money in itself is the root of all evil; and this idolatry can possess us with terrible ease if we fail to maintain Christ's wisdom about it in ourselves.—1972

MAY 30

John 16:12-13. *I still have many things to say to you, but you cannot bear them now. When the Spirit of truth comes, he will guide you into all the truth.*

When Jesus ended his earthly mission, he still had "many things to say" to his disciples which they were not then ready to receive. Yet such things need not become the lost words of Jesus if we permit the Spirit of truth to guide us into "all the truth."

Note what this means and what it does not mean. The New Testament writers were inspired and led by God, yet they never pretended to be infallible. Saint Paul admitted that not everything he wrote carried divine authority: "I have no command of the Lord, but I give my opinion...and I think that I too have the Spirit of God" (1 Corinthians 7:25, 40).

Would that all Christians were so modest and so honest! No person or church can claim infallibility or a monopoly on divine truth. It is enough that God promises to reveal to those who humbly seek the guidance of the Holy Spirit all that they need to know of him and of his saving love. May the whole church of Christ be led into a more humble and faithful surrender to God's will.—1951

MAY 31

Luke 1:46. *And Mary said, "My soul magnifies the Lord."*

Mary's willing obedience to God brought her intense pain and unutterable joy. Centuries of Christian piety can be a stumbling block to a true appreciation of her courageous "yes" to God. A young peasant girl from the backwater of Galilee, engaged but not yet married to Joseph, became pregnant and undoubtedly suffered the shame and humiliation of slanderous misunderstanding. Her song of joy, the Magnificat, is a daring expression of faith and hope in God, who turns normal expectations upside down.

Mary is among the anwim, the poor for whom God especially has compassion. Saint Luke records numerous stories of people in this category—lepers, children, women, Samaritans—all of whom are powerless. The song captures a vision of hope, the expectation that however oppressive the present may seem, the strong do not have the last word. Mary, who raised Jesus during his formative years and then watched him slip away from her as his vocation took him toward the cross, embraced life with all its ambiguity. All generations, including our own, rightly call her blessed.—1989

JUNE

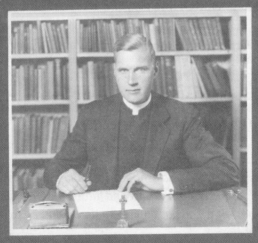

August-October 1984

FORWARD
Day by Day

*"to prepare and carry out
definite plans... for an
organized effort to reinvigorate
the life of the church
and to rehabilitate its general,
diocesan and parochial work"*

JUNE 1

Psalm 45:7. *Your throne, O God, endures for ever and ever.*

Psalm 45 celebrates the institution of Davidic kingship in Israel and at the same time the ultimate reign of God. The pageantry described in the psalm enables people to look beyond human power to God, whose throne is eternal.

We are reminded daily of the struggle between the powers of this world and often hear their claims to ultimate truth. It is good to recall, even as we commit ourselves to the cause of peace and justice, that God reigns above all. We may get a glimpse of the epiphany of our Creator; our faith is strengthened each time that happens—sometimes in the unlikeliest places.

The psalm provides a panorama of God's activity and human experience. Undergirding everything, the unshakable, eternal God remains faithful. Our God reigns, and so we do all in our power to bring about the peace of the world, to make it visible to all. In the process we learn to trust divine faithfulness even when fear threatens to overwhelm.—1989

JUNE 2

Ecclesiastes 3:11. *[God] has made everything suitable for its time; moreover he has put a sense of past and future into their minds, yet they cannot find out what God has done from the beginning to the end.*

The world God has made and in which he has placed us is indeed "suitable"—and beautiful, challenging, irritating, enjoyable, fragile, and many other things. But because God has also put into our minds "a sense of past and future," we cannot be content with this present world as all-sufficient and all there is. There is more than we can see. We are baffled by the mystery of our existence because we know we do not see everything—much of the past has been unnoted or forgotten, and we can only guess the future. We "cannot find out what God has done from the beginning to the end." And then there is eternity, which is beyond past, present, and future. What is that?

Jesus said, "Whoever has seen me has seen the Father" (John 14:9). We need look no further than Jesus. Jesus is eternity in time. He is the answer God gives us. We will not understand everything in this life, and probably not in the next. Much will ever be beyond our understanding. But Jesus we know, and that knowledge is sufficient for us.—1959

JUNE 3

Psalm 8:5. *What is man that you should be mindful of him? the son of man that you should seek him out?*

It is not just your neighbor who is created in the image of God. You, too, are made in his image and likeness. This means that you must not underestimate your own value and your own dignity. Some people do. They say, "Oh, I don't make much difference. What I do is of little consequence." That is not true. We are each to love ourselves and see our own worth by the clear commandment of Christ. We are to love our neighbors as we love ourselves.

We must have a true estimate of our own dignity. It is the surest defense against temptation. If we are tempted to do a cheap thing, we must say, "This is not the way the image of God should behave."

Each person is a coin made in God's mint and stamped with his likeness. We possess immortal souls and minds that can understand the workings of the stars. We are the sons and daughters of God. Let us not underestimate ourselves. Do not leave the winning of others to Christ to someone whose power you respect. You have influence and power of your own. Do what you can, and keep on.—1952

JUNE 4

Matthew 14:26. *When the disciples saw him walking on the sea, they were terrified, saying, "It is a ghost!"*

Of course, we enlightened children of the twentieth century don't believe in ghosts, and we can look quite patronizingly at those poor terrified Galilean primitives who did. But then—have you ever been in a boat on a rough sea, looked out over the waves, and seen your best friend calmly walking toward you on the surface of the water? If you haven't, don't be too sure about what you would think or say if you did.

Let's give that cry of the disciples a parabolic interpretation. They saw Jesus and thought he was a ghost. Don't many people look at Jesus today and think he is a ghost—an unreal figure, an apparition from another world of reality? They may see him as a beautiful ghost rather than a frightening one, but a ghost, nonetheless: somebody not quite real, too good to be true.

Whether we find Jesus beautiful or frightening, whether we like him or love him or dislike him or detest him, how real to us is he?

Christ becomes real to people in just one way. He becomes real to those who think and live as if he were the ultimate reality of their lives. He is real to us in direct proportion of our being in earnest as his followers.—1976

JUNE 5

Luke 6:20. *Then he looked up at his disciples and said: "Blessed are you who are poor, for yours is the kingdom of God."*

She offered the gift in a plastic grocery bag. Money is tight this year, so we decided to give our friends what we had. She smiled apologetically. Inside the bag was five pounds of beef wrapped in butcher paper. And I came to our appointment empty-handed. I didn't have a present; it didn't occur to me to bring one.

Our relationship is customer and service provider—I visit her every six weeks or so, and she works her magic. Our conversations are easy and deep, though we have little in common on the surface: She grew up the last child in a big family, with an alcoholic father who left when she was an infant. Pregnant early, divorced from an abusive husband, estranged from her daughter and son, she is a woman of deep and abiding faith who thanks God often in our conversations and wrestles with God's plan for her life. I am solidly middle class, with a husband and two children, a dog, a horse, and a rabbit, living in a nice house in a good neighborhood.

Jesus reminds us that poverty does not determine generosity, that the poor have much to offer, and the saints of God often come from the least expected places.—2016

JUNE 6

Luke 7:13. *Do not weep.*

Jesus said that. He was speaking to a widow whose only son had just died. Reading those three words of Jesus, I can almost feel his calm. I want that.

I'm not dead. I am, however, seemingly stuck in prison. About a month before I began writing these meditations, I received some hopeful news: I may get out. I'm guilty of first-degree manslaughter, but was convicted of and sentenced for murder. A recent court ruling may right this, maybe before I finish writing these meditations. I wasn't going to mention it because, well, I'm not sure what the outcome will be and if I tell you about it and then it doesn't happen, what kind of faith story is that? In all the gospel stories, it seems that once Jesus arrives on the scene, storms are calmed, sickness healed, and the dead raised. I want a happy ending for my story, too.

So, what happens if this judge sees things differently than I do? What happens if it turns out I am to stay in prison? What then? That's not a happy ending like we read in the gospels. But Jesus said, "Do not weep." I'm going to try that.—1998

JUNE 7

Galatians 4:15. *What has become of the goodwill you felt?*

Paul is struggling with the Christians in Galatia. He had put a lot of himself into these congregations, preaching the gospel to them. But now the passion and the love they exhibited at first is fading, and Paul is hurt and upset.

Growing up together as a community in Christ wasn't easy then and it is not easy now. Matters of faith go deep—to the very heart of people's lives and their identities. The struggles that occur within the church are always passionate. But that is why we all need to remember what makes the church unique. It is a covenant community. In Christ we make a commitment to one another, and we make every effort to keep the commitment. We do this so that we won't give up on one another as we struggle to understand our faith and its meaning in our lives.

A character in a film once remarked that "making new friends was easy, but making old friends took a lot of work." The same goes for the church. It's easy to fall in love with a new-found faith, but when the questions and struggles come, it takes commitment to hang in there with our brothers and sisters who are struggling too. —2000

JUNE 8

Psalm 62:12. *Put no trust in extortion; in robbery take no empty pride.*

For three years I taught at an international private school in England. Over time, I realized the school was being run as a money-making enterprise. Students were suffering in their studies as a result. Most of them were boarders from a distant country. Few parents actually witnessed the deteriorating condition of the school.

I felt caught in the middle: having and voicing concerns about various immoral aspects of the school, but going with the flow to protect my job. My conversations with school administrators were difficult. In the end, it was obvious I was getting nowhere, so I left the school.

In our working lives it is critical that we make clear the fundamental tenets of our faith and stick to them. All around us we see the hypocritical and even evil actions of those sunk in greed or a lust for power. In working with and deriving our income from such people we become part of the problem instead of part of the solution, and in essence become recipients of "stolen goods."

Blow whistles, question authority; but above all ask God to guide you toward work which glorifies his kingdom rather than the fallen world.—2003

JUNE 9

Matthew 16:4. *No sign will be given to it except the sign of Jonah.*

Jesus here expresses his impatience with those who want a sign. He is impatient because they are surrounded with signs—God's creative glory, his love, his word, his continuing presence—all the signs they could want or need.

Yet Jesus says the sign of Jonah will be given. The church has long taken this to mean his own resurrection after three days, but there is another possible meaning as well. Jonah's resurrection is clearly a sign. But so also is the whole saga of the Book of Jonah, which tells the story of the redemption of nations. In it, Ninevah is saved. Outsiders repent and receive God's mercy. Think of that "sign of Jonah" in terms of Jesus' saving act and the spread of the blessed company of all the faithful to the ends of the earth by means of it. Think of Jesus' Great Commission at the end of this gospel: "Go therefore and make disciples of all nations."

If the Spirit of God should once again hover like a dove over the face of all the waters as it did at the creation, if God should then "become king over all the earth" (Zechariah 14:9), is that not the "sign of Jonah," and is that not what Jesus would desire?—1979

JUNE 10

Matthew 16:17. *And Jesus answered him, "Blessed are you, Simon son of Jonah! For flesh and blood has not revealed this to you, but my Father in heaven."*

"Then he sternly ordered the disciples not to tell anyone that he was the Messiah." Has this passage maddened you, as it has me? If God reveals a truth, why tell no one? Is this not the direct opposite of the Great Commission in Matthew 28:19: "Go therefore and make disciples of all nations"?

My own first flicker of understanding came with the reading of Psalm 51, a masterpiece of Hebrew parallelism, in which the poetry consists of saying the same truth twice: "Wash me through and through...and cleanse me from my sin." And, "For I know my transgressions, and my sin is ever before me." Then, in verse 7: "For behold, you look for truth deep within me, and will make me understand wisdom secretly."

Aha! "Secretly" means "deep within me." I am no good as a messenger if my grasp of truth is superficial. Truth must reach and work upon my secret places before it is fully mine, before I have all of me to offer. The disciples must tell no one until their own fears and doubts and hesitancies are purified by Jesus' offering. Then they can go, filled with all power, into all the world.—1979

JUNE 11

Acts 11:24. *For [Barnabas] was a good man, full of the Holy Spirit and of faith. And a great many people were brought to the Lord.*

It is not said that many people were brought to the Lord because Barnabas was the kind of Christian that he was, but it is implicit— and it is most plausible. There is only one kind of evangelism, of winning people to Christ, that is effective in the long run. It is the evangelism of example and witness. People will want to become Christians when they see that people like Barnabas are Christians.

This man truly adorned the doctrine of the Lord Jesus Christ by being loving, caring, outreaching, in the way of his divine Master. And so—large numbers were won over to the Lord.

John Greenleaf Whittier wrote of a friend:

The dear Lord's best interpreters
Are humble human souls;
The Gospel of a life like hers
Is more than books or scrolls.

It is ever so. And if in our day we want the church to grow in numbers, we must understand that we who are the church must first grow in grace, so that people will want to become what we are. —1972

JUNE 12

Matthew 17:4. *Then Peter said to Jesus, "Lord, it is good for us to be here; if you wish, I will make three dwellings here, one for you, one for Moses, and one for Elijah."*

When we enjoy a good experience, we often try to prolong it or to repeat it. With religious experience we may try to stay on a spiritual high by having progressively more intense experiences. If we do so we become religious "addicts" on an ego trip rather than on the path of being open to God's direction.

In the gospel lesson, Peter tries to do just that. He wants to stay on the mountain where they had seen Jesus transfigured. Jesus led them off the mountain to go on his journey toward Jerusalem and the events which were to happen there.

Spiritual highs are a delight when they happen, much as a sunny day when we are not expecting it. But to focus on them distracts from getting on with our journey. It would be like staying at a party too long in the hope that something more might happen.

There is a time to stay, and a time to go and get on with something else.—1990

JUNE 13

Luke 7:47. *Therefore, I tell you, her sins, which were many, have been forgiven; hence she has shown great love. But the one to whom little is forgiven, loves little.*

Jesus was at table at the home of a Pharisee. A woman known to be a sinner came in, bathed Jesus' feet with her tears, dried them with her hair, kissed and then anointed them with costly ointment. The Pharisee thought Jesus would realize her sinfulness and avoid her. Instead, Jesus pointed out in contrast that the Pharisee had not offered him any water to wash off the dirt. "Her sins…have been forgiven; hence she has shown great love."

Duty can guide us in moments of temptation; laws can instruct us in the conduct that God desires and the world needs. But what can reach our wills and get action is grateful love born of forgiveness.

How can we live like saints, as the real friends of Jesus? How can we help God's kingdom to come?

A former missionary to China tells of an elderly man who came asking for baptism. The missionary asked why he sought to change his faith. The answer was: "My religion instructs my head; yours makes the feet go."

The secret of the saints is the grateful love that lives to proclaim the great things God has done for us.—1947

JUNE 14

Matthew 17:20. *[Jesus] said to them, "Because of your little faith. For truly I tell you, if you have faith the size of a mustard seed, you will say to this mountain, 'Move from here to there,' and it will move; and nothing will be impossible for you."*

Late one Friday afternoon, a priest received a phone call from a woman he did not know, who needed almost $2,000 by Monday afternoon or she and her family would be homeless. Various illnesses had kept the woman and her husband from working, and they were months behind in their mortgage payments. The woman was a member of no church and seemed to have no interest in changing that: she simply wanted money, and her situation was desperate. The priest offered her what he could, but it was not enough to stop the foreclosure. He could not get the plight of this family of six out of his mind.

Early on Sunday morning he decided to tell the parish that the loose offering that day would go to help some strangers keep their house. Because it was a holiday weekend and many people were out of town, he did not know what to expect. But when the loose offering was counted, it amounted to just over $2,000.

Jesus' words about faith moving mountains have gotten a lot of people into trouble because they relied on a miracle to do everything. What Jesus means is that generosity of spirit always accomplishes more than too scrupulous insistence on what cannot be done.
—2003

JUNE 15

Romans 1:16. *For I am not ashamed of the gospel; it is the power of God for salvation to everyone who has faith, to the Jew first and also to the Greek.*

The Jews and the Greeks thought the early Christians were stupid for believing in a crucified Savior. But far from being ashamed of this belief, Saint Paul made it the heart of his gospel, and gloried in it as containing a revelation of the love of God which had in it "the power of God for salvation" for all people.

There is no stumbling block in the idea of a crucified Savior today. But there is still need for this upstanding attitude of Saint Paul's in the witness of Christians to Christ. Does a sneer make us cowards? Or the fear of unpopularity keeps us silent about our faith?
—1969

JUNE 16

Romans 1:28. *Since they did not see fit to acknowledge God, God gave them up to a debased mind and to things that should not be done.*

Why do you suppose people to whom God has given an innate knowledge and awareness of himself "see fit" to rid their minds of that knowledge and choose for themselves a mind minus that knowledge? One explanation is that such people (and they seem to include just about everybody) want freedom from the knowledge that we are born to serve and obey God rather than our own selves. To that rejection of God from our mind, heart, and primary concern, Paul attributes all the pain and woe of this perishing world.

Who will say that he is wrong? Yet who among us can say that we do not have to struggle with the temptation to dismiss God from mind whenever his presence there seems to threaten what we consider our God-given freedom to be ourselves?

I have been reading a new book about C. S. Lewis in which someone who knew him well reports hearing him say: "I was not born to be free—I was born to adore and to obey." He knew the truth of the paradox that in God's service is perfect freedom. Let us know it too and hold God ever in our minds in adoring love. —1986

JUNE 17

Psalm 85:8. *I will listen to what the Lord God is saying, for he is speaking peace to his faithful people and to those who turn their hearts to him.*

Though you probably don't say these words at breakfast on Sunday morning, you could—and their energy might take you right to church; open your ears to prayer, hymn, and sermon; sign you up to teach Sunday school; even get you back there for the Tuesday night Bible study.

God's speaking will not be limited, though, to churches. Once we are ready to hear, God will use the most mundane moment at the office, a chance encounter with a stranger, even our own image in the bathroom mirror, to teach us, to "speak peace" to us. The peace of which, and with which, God will speak may not comfort. It may distinctly discomfort, painfully prick our conscience, drive us to sacrifice confident prejudice for risky tolerance, even force us out into yet another battle with old familiar evils. God's peace can move us into forgiving, even loving, a cherished enemy. God's peace may empty our bank account, open our spare bedroom, fill our days off, amaze us, delight us.

God's peace-speaking will open our ears and turn our hearts to hear more. May the energy of that peace recreate us in God's image, ready to do God's will.—1996

JUNE 18

Matthew 18:21-22. *Then Peter came and said to him, "Lord, if another member of the church sins against me, how often should I forgive? As many as seven times?" Jesus said to him, "Not seven times, but, I tell you, seventy-seven times.*

Resentments boomerang. A harsh word may hurt you once, but each time you recall it, you stab yourself. Resentment blocks faith in God, for unforgiveness cannot understand and accept forgiveness. It mocks the Lord's Prayer. Do you pray to forgive but never forget, to forgive but never to want to see the offender again?

Jesus on the cross prayed, "Father, forgive them for they know not what they do." Can anyone's wrongs match those he forgave? How can one forgive great wrong? Prayer for the offender is one remedy. God often gives understanding that changes hatred to pity. As the French say, "To understand all is to forgive all." Or pray for God's spirit of forgiveness.

A young woman, deeply wronged by a friend, forgave but could not get rid of the hurt. She asked God to put his forgiveness in her heart. Then she had a dream of a dark well in which a tiny shaft of light spread until all darkness was gone. When she awoke no hurt remained.—1943

JUNE 19

Romans 3:9. *Are we any better off? No, not at all; for we have already charged that all, both Jews and Greeks, are under the power of sin.*

Our prisons are full of men and women who have been told they were bad for as long as they can remember. Though you don't have to be in prison to know people who will tell you how, all their life, someone—maybe everyone—told them they'd never amount to anything, that they were worthless, miserable, stupid, ugly, dirty.

What do they call it? Original sin? Why not just Born Bad? What good can come out of a belief in an inherent dirtiness? Don't get me wrong—I'm all for admitting our powerlessness and limitations, even our darkness. I know that, without God, I am nothing. I understand the thinking behind this doctrine and I agree with the part of it that says we need God. We do. Badly.

However, there is another doctrine, not so widely circulated. Its Latin name is imago Dei. It focuses on our being made in the image of God. What about that? We like to say, "I'm only human," as a means of excusing our mistakes. What if, instead, we picked ourselves up, dusted off the seat of our pants, and said, "I'll get this right. After all, I'm imprinted with the divine"?

Most of us already know how bad we are. We need to learn how good we are.—2002

JUNE 20

John 13:33. *Little children, I am with you only a little longer.*

My children are both now in college. Since they were young, my parting words to them have always been "I love you." Headed to kindergarten. Off to summer camp. To a friend's to play. These days, it's the final salutation of text messages.

In this passage from John, we remember Jesus' final hours with his friends. A lot is packed into one evening: the foot washing, the

Lord's Supper, the command to love one another, the betrayal, the arrest. And Jesus is saying goodbye.

Most of us have said goodbye to someone we love. It might have been at the deathbed or at the end of a relationship. It can be heartbreaking. The word goodbye can leave a vacant place in our hearts that is never filled.

Did the disciples get the chance to say goodbye, or were they haunted later by the things they never said? When they got to the Mount of Olives, did they realize these were their precious final hours with him? Did they know that Judas' kiss of greeting was a goodbye masquerading as a hello?

Whether it was stated aloud or communicated through a long and loving look, I think I know Jesus' parting words: I love you. —2015

🙚🙘🙚🙘

JUNE 21

Romans 3:22-24. *For there is no distinction, since all have sinned and fall short of the glory of God; they are justified by his grace as a gift, through the redemption that is in Christ Jesus.*

Most of us are not notorious evil-doers, but it may come as a shock to realize that we are not perfect. "Oh, I'm not a sinner—sinners commit murder and cheat and are slimy characters," we may say. But then we are not Jesus either—he was perfect. And yes, we have sinned, and then probably within seconds of having our sins forgiven in church on Sunday morning, have sinned once again in thought, mind, and maybe even deed.

Receiving the gift of grace, bought for us through the death of Jesus Christ, is often difficult. In giving a gift we are in control; in receiving a gift someone else is. Poor receivers, we are often loath to accept a gift, a compliment, even love itself. Grace is a free gift. We do nothing to earn it—we can't—with good works, money, or success. We do have to ask for it—and for many of us it is difficult to know even that we need it. There is such a thing as a "free lunch." It is called the grace of God.—2004

JUNE 22

Matthew 19:27. *Peter said in reply, "Look, we have left everything and followed you. What then will we have?"*

What Peter wanted to know is the question we still ask today. How shall we know that we have found God? What results may we expect to find due to our contact with God? Let us not fall into the dangerous mistake of supposing that it is primarily a matter of our emotions, of whether we "feel" God near or not.

If we, by an act of imaginative faith, put out the trembling hands of our spirit to touch God, we may expect first of all a changed attitude to life. As the poet Tennyson described God, "Closer is he than breathing, and nearer than hands and feet."

Having accepted God as our pilot, we will let our ship of life go whither God directs. Upon new attitude must follow new action. It is in the doing of God's will that we find assurance of God's presence. With new action come new relationships—and new sufferings! We will be taking care of duties and of persons formerly ignored or neglected. We will be making amends to those we hurt. And we now will receive new hurts and bear them without resentment for Christ's sake.

No one can foretell our new life, but in it all God will prove himself very near.—1939

JUNE 23

Matthew 20:13. *Friend, I am doing you no wrong.*

It is certainly not just or fair that those who had worked for twelve hours should receive the same pay as those who had worked only one. Then why did our Lord tell this story?

The key word which unlocks the mystery of the parable is friend. We expect to hear the word laborer or employee. Such a word we could understand.

But then we should have lost the point of the parable. This is no lesson in economics, but a call to friendship. To all who seek to enter into relations with God on the basis of merit and contract, God's chosen ways of grace and friendship will seem unjust. But God will not permit us to have relations with him on the basis of merit. He would lift our relations to a higher level—that of friendship. With friends we do not keep accounts of merit. Friendship recognizes no limits of giving.

Has God dealt with you on the basis of merit or friendship? Do you want God to deal with others as he has dealt with you?—1946

JUNE 24

Luke 1:68-69, 71. *Blessed be the Lord God of Israel, for he has looked favorably on his people and redeemed them. He has raised up a mighty savior for us in the house of his servant David…that we would be saved from our enemies and from the hand of all who hate us.*

We are all lonely. God has made each one of us to be different. No one has ever looked out upon this life with my eyes. No one can enter my world, except for a little way by sympathy. No one can bear my burdens. Not even my dearest ones understand the whole of me. I do not understand myself. Here I stand upon this ball of earth speeding through space, surrounded by my brothers and sisters, yet, like some bewildered child upon the city streets, a solitary, lonely being.

Where shall we find the answer to our loneliness? In the presence of God. Jesus once said to his disciples, "I am not alone because the Father is with me" (John 16:32). The man who keeps himself continually in God's promised presence is never lonely. True worship brings us together out of our loneliness and makes us at home in the companionship of God our Father. Therefore we can sing with real joy: "Blessed be the Lord God…for he has looked favorably on his people and redeemed them."—1937

JUNE 25

Matthew 20:34. *Jesus touched their eyes. Immediately they regained their sight and followed him.*

Hatred is a weak vice. It distorts our view of the world, of our neighbor (or "enemy"), and of ourselves. The strength of forgiveness on the other hand is the true view it opens up. We begin to see things as they really are, in the sight of God. We begin to see our neighbor—even his weaknesses and failings—with the eyes of God. The things we hated about him fall into true perspective, and we begin to wonder at the way God is leading him to something better. Then we begin to want to help him. And ourselves we see for what we are—equally poor sinners in God's sight with the persons we once disliked.

It has been said that sorrow cleanses the eyes that they may more clearly see. That is even truer of forgiveness. Forgiveness is our most God-like quality, and the one that brings us nearest to the divine presence. As was said of the ancient Rabbi Hillel, "His loving-kindness brought men close under the wings of 'Shekinah,'"(that is, into the presence of God). Such grace, Paul tells us in Romans 5:21, will lead us to eternal life through Jesus Christ.—1938

JUNE 26

Romans 6:4. *Just as Christ was raised from the dead by the glory of the Father, so we too might walk in newness of life.*

The Athenians thought Saint Paul was talking about two gods, one named Jesus and the other named the resurrection—a heartbreaking experience for the preacher. The mistake persists.

There are those who believe in Jesus but not in the resurrection. They mean to follow him even though they have no hope of anything at the end but a sense of duty well done. They are apt to say that they accept the Golden Rule and the Sermon on the Mount, and even the cross as the world's most heroic example of self-giving, but beyond that, "We must not trust in imponderables."

On the other hand, there are those who believe in the resurrection but not in Jesus. They expect a continuance of existence no matter how good or bad they have been. Newman's sermon, "Holiness necessary for future blessedness," is dismissed as old-fashioned.

Jesus and the resurrection are inseparable. "If Christ has not been raised, your faith is futile....If for this life only we have hoped in Christ, we are of all people most to be pitied" (1 Corinthians 15:17-19).—1954

JUNE 27

Luke 9:51. *[Jesus] set his face to go to Jerusalem.*

The phrase "set his face" is a powerful image. It speaks of determination and courage. There are times when it is clear what we must do. We have to grit our teeth (maybe that's what causes the face to set) and do it. We admire people who have that clarity and sometimes envy them because we do not feel that clearly about what we are to do.

The paradox is that we must be confused for a time before we can be clear. We have to dip our bucket into the depths of doubt and confusion before we pull it up to the surface light of clear decision. It's much like inhaling and exhaling. Those who try to be clear all the time without dipping into the courage of their uncertainties can become shallow. No one can, or should, be clear all the time. It is like baking a cake—in the beginning there is only a mess of ingredients. It's supposed to be that way.

For Jesus to have been so clear about what he had to do in Jerusalem, he must have had many agonizing days in prayer and uncertainty about what God wanted him to do. He must have had to dip deeply into that well.—1995

JUNE 28

Matthew 21:12-13. *Jesus entered the temple and drove out all who were selling and buying in the temple, and he overturned the tables of the money changers and the seats of those who sold doves. He said to them, "It is written, 'My house shall be called a house of prayer'; but you are making it a den of robbers."*

Bible reading can be a drab and uninteresting experience, but not if we read in an understanding manner. For example, read the story of the cleansing of the temple. As I read that story recently these words came to life and jumped out at me and seemed to say: "This is for you. Take it and use it." Here are the words: "My house shall be called a house of prayer."

Jesus was referring to the temple, to be sure; but we can apply it to ourselves. My house, my home—is it a place of prayer? Is there a consciousness of God's presence as we live together as a family? Or has the day already been spoiled because selfish desires have come in to push aside God's love, which can be expressed only in our love for each other?

Three signs of a house of prayer:

There is thoughtfulness each for the other.

There is temper control because God is in control.

There is infinite patience.—1971

JUNE 29

John 21:17. *Feed my sheep.*

Saint Peter and Saint Paul, whose ministries permeated the entire Gentile and Jewish world of their day, have been associated in the devotional life of the Christian church since earliest times. Their joint feast is one of the oldest saints' days on the calendar, observed since the year 258.

Reliable tradition has fixed Peter's martyrdom (he was crucified upside down) in Rome around the year 64. Paul is in Rome as the

Book of Acts ends. He may have traveled to Spain after that, but tradition says he returned to Rome, where he was beheaded during Nero's persecution.

Perhaps we can examine today our own openness toward Christians of other persuasions, for this day has an ecumenical message, commemorating in one celebration the central figure of the Roman Catholic tradition, Peter, and the apostle whose teaching was of bedrock importance for the churches of the Reformation, Paul. —1985

JUNE 30

Romans 7:15. *I do not understand my own actions.*

Paul is at his best when he is most personal—as he is here. In fact, we all bear witness best to our faith when we speak out of our own experience. So Paul, having used scripture and reason to illustrate the power of sin in human life, now looks into his own struggle and tells us, in one of the most moving passages in all his writing, the agony he experiences when he confronts himself.

Is this your experience also? "I do not do the good I want, but the evil I do not want is what I do…Wretched man that I am!"

There in a nutshell is the whole tragedy of the human story. Think of the United States in Vietnam, setting out to do good and save a nation from communism but causing untold suffering instead. Think of parents who want so desperately for their children to do good that they drive them to rebellion. Think of ourselves, wanting to follow Christ, yet losing our tempers, failing to pray, not following through. If we're honest, we must ask with Paul, "Who will deliver me from this body of death?"

If we have really looked into ourselves and agonized as Paul did over what we found, we can rejoice with Paul in the answer: "Thanks be to God through Jesus Christ our Lord!"—1995

JULY

JULY 1

Matthew 22:2. *The kingdom of heaven may be compared to a king who gave a wedding banquet for his son.*

One Sunday a month our parish serves a meal to homeless women. Last time, my nine-year-old daughter came along. She jumped at the chance—anything to get away from her little brother. As we drove into the "badlands" of our city, I thought she might be a little young for this kind of thing. But at the homeless shelter, she found her place in the serving line and poured juice for a few hundred guests. I glanced at her now and again, and she seemed fine. We didn't say much on the way home. My thoughts were already elsewhere.

The next day was her birthday, and birthdays are always a big deal at our house—presents and singing, friends and family, a real feast. When I put my daughter to bed, I asked her what had been the most special part of the celebration. "The meal," she said. We had ordered pizza. "But we have pizza all the time," I said.

"Not that meal," she said. "The meal for the ladies, the meal where I poured the juice. That was my favorite part."

She had not missed the feast that God had put before her. Maybe the next time, I won't either.—2004

❧❧❧

JULY 2

Psalm 141:3. *Set a watch before my mouth, O Lord, and guard the door of my lips.*

One of my ongoing prayers is for the strength to curb my tongue and not offer my marvelous insights on everything. This does not mean that I must always be silent, but it does mean that I must listen and be sensitive to the needs and feelings of other people before I speak. Most especially, it means that I am called to listen, prayerfully and attentively, for the voice of God.

Norvene Vest in *No Moment Too Small* says that "before we speak, we can choose silence and then look honestly at what the urge to speak is telling us about ourselves." That is good advice.

Must I have an opinion on everything? If I do have an opinion, must I belabor it? Is that clever retort necessary? Will my speech hurt someone? Am I really listening to my friend, my partner, my children? Do I ask or demand too much? Am I content to sit silently in God's presence and listen instead of always asking? God speaks to us in the silence within us. I must guard against blocking out God's voice with the noise of my own voice.—1999

JULY 3

Matthew 22:39. *You shall love your neighbor as yourself.*

This second of the great commandments presented by Jesus assumes that we love ourselves—and it does not challenge that love. Loving someone else is a virtual impossibility without a healthy love of ourselves.

On the face of it, the idea seems presumptuous. What right have we to love ourselves? Especially on days when things go wrong, when our failures far outnumber our successes, our mistakes obliterate our achievements, we wonder what there can be about us that could be lovable. Yet God accepts us and loves us. What right have we to consider ourselves better judges of humanity than God?

"Self-acquaintance is a rare condition," Robert Henri said. And even more rare, perhaps, is self-acceptance. If we try to see ourselves as we really are, we may find that some of our most endearing qualities are our faults. We must not hate ourselves because of our faults; we must love ourselves in spite of them, and with the kind of love God has for us: not an admiring approval, but a merciful willingness to accept and live with imperfection and failure.—1962

JULY 4

Galatians 6:14. *May I never boast of anything except the cross of our Lord Jesus Christ by which the Lord has been crucified to me, and I to the world.*

There is a beloved hymn that begins, "When I survey the wondrous cross." The word "survey" means "to look at." There is great value in simply looking at a cross or crucifix. We hear much about visual education these days. The church has used symbolism for generations. The cross is one of the most effective kinds of visual education.

For Christians the cross is a very powerful symbol. Simply to look at it for five minutes can be of great help. It helps fix our minds on what Christ did for us. It helps get our minds off ourselves and centered on our Lord. As we look at the cross, we will probably think about the great sacrifice of himself that Christ made for us. We will be deeply grateful for this. We may reflect that we are called upon to take up our cross and follow him. Our burdens become lighter as we look at the cross. The cross is a powerful symbol of a mighty fact. Look at it, and see what God says to you as you gaze.—1975

JULY 5

Deuteronomy 10:19. *You shall also love the stranger, for you were strangers in the land of Egypt.*

Let it be recalled at each Independence Day that Americans, like the Israelites of old, have come out of oppression and bondage in their "Egypt"—Europe originally, but now from elsewhere as well—into a land of freedom, flowing with milk and honey (and let us not forget the underside of this story—our ancestors dispossessing the innocent natives of their land and freedom). The author of our reading from Deuteronomy was a Hebrew theologian who reflected on God's character: "a great God, mighty and awesome, who is not partial and takes no bribe" and "loves the strangers, providing them food and clothing."

Nowadays we hear too many Americans talking about recent refugees and migrants from other lands as if they had forgotten that their own ancestors were once strangers in the land of Egypt. God willed that his people should be free some three thousand years ago. He willed that our ancestors should be free. He wills that we share our freedom and abundance in this good land with all who long for it and will try to use freedom well. God bless America, that she may never shut her doors to those who are free in hope and in spirit. —1983

JULY 6

Romans 8:35, 37. *Who will separate us from the love of Christ? Will hardship, or distress, or persecution, or famine, or nakedness, or peril, or sword?…No, in all these things we are more than conquerors through him who loved us.*

Albert Einstein some time ago said he had always thought that when the crisis came in Germany, the universities would be the bulwark of human freedom; but when the crisis did come, in the face of a grim and utterly ruthless government, the universities capitulated and collapsed, and it is the Christian church that has kept alive whatever of freedom is left there.

The crisis will come for all of us in one form or another. If we depend on our own abilities—though we be intellectual giants—we shall fail. Loyal members of the church find a strength which gives them victory. Are we now proving our loyalty as church members?

"The church is the only organism within a nation which by its very nature must be loyal to a God beyond the state, to humanity beyond the nation, to the kingdom of God beyond any actual social order," said theologian John C. Bennett.

In any conflict between loyalty to Christ and any other loyalty, Christ claims our allegiance.—1937

JULY 7

Matthew 23:37. *How often have I desired to gather your children together as a hen gathers her brood under her wings, and you were not willing!*

I grew up on a farm. As a child, I was assigned to feed the chickens. The chickens were not possessed of great intelligence. They ran hither and yon, especially the young chicks. The hens spent most of their time trying to round up their brood, one of whom would always head off in some contrary direction. The hen would try to keep the rest together while seeking the errant chick.

The chicks rebelled at being held close or led, until something was amiss. A loud noise, impending rain, or the sound of a coyote would send them scurrying to get under the hen's wings. Then, it seemed, the wings that were never large enough to encircle the entire brood when they were jostling about would expand and cover them all. Small, fearful, hunkered down, the chicks sat in the protection of those wings.

The portrait is not flattering to us, but having seen chicks and hens, I know it is accurate. I mostly keep trying to go my own way, until some event sends me scurrying for the right place, the place it is my nature to inhabit—the warmth and safety of God's expansive embrace.—2002

JULY 8

Psalm 18:20. *He brought me out into an open place; he rescued me because he delighted in me.*

Psalm 18 is filled with gratitude for what God has done in the psalmist's life. Over and over the biblical story depicts a saving God, a rescuing God who comes to take people out of harm's way and to restore their lives, to give them peace. The Bible makes plain that it is at the heart of the divine character to save. What is not often said is that this characteristic act of saving occurs because of delight. The psalmist who composed Psalm 18 declares he was brought "out into an open place" and rescued because God "delighted in me."

God does not simply tolerate us. God does not only pity us. God delights in us, finds pleasure in us, seeks us out to save us because we give him joy.

Consider that you are God's joy, that God seeks you out to save you because God delights in you. God wants you to let him bring you into "an open place," a place without the confining walls of doubt and fear and hopelessness, a place full of light where you will know that God put you there for the sublime reason that God delights in you. —1995

❦❦❦

JULY 9

Psalm 22:9. *Yet you are he who took me out of the womb, and kept me safe upon my mother's breast.*

God, it feels that you have forsaken me. Our ancestors trusted in you and you delivered them; but people look on me as a worm, and you ignore me as though I didn't exist.

But it was you who brought me into the world. When I sucked my mother's milk, I was acting on that life-impulse that animates all your creatures, the hope you planted in me. And so, while my desolate heart tells me that you have abandoned me, my mind clings to the thought that you brought me into this life and bid me now to live and trust you to bring me through. If I am nothing, it is because you created me to be nothing, and I know that cannot be.

Thus thought this troubled psalmist of long ago. This psalm was also our Lord's "song in the night" on his cross. And it is healing medicine for us whenever we feel less than nothing in God's world. God brought us into this life. Shall he not see us through it? Read this psalm carefully, read it whole, and when you need a song in your night, turn to it.—1981

JULY 10

Psalm 116:9. *I believed, even when I said, "I have been brought very low."*

We had gotten engaged, but I hadn't told my parents. Their household was in turmoil due to my mother's radiation therapy and chemotherapy. We arrived at my parents' home, with the engagement ring in prominent but unspoken display. My mother may have been ill, but she was still sharp. "Nice ring," she said, glowing.

My mother spent much of the next several days with her soon-to-be daughter-in-law, telling her everything, passing on the entire wisdom of the tribe. I think she knew she was bound for glory and would not live until our wedding—but we weren't ready for that. She needed to dispense a lifetime of mother-in-lawing first.

She was in pain, and brought low. There was no comfortable position for her; when given enough medication for relief, she slept. "Time is short and the water rises," she would often say, and then refuse medication.

My fiancée's parents had died; my mother would be crossing over soon. She asked my fiancée if there was anything she wanted to tell them, for she was convinced she would be seeing them soon, just as she knew she would be seeing her Lord. Even brought low, she believed.—1999

JULY 11

Luke 10:34. *He put him on his own animal, and brought him to an inn, and took care of him.*

In the parable of the Good Samaritan there is one character who is usually overlooked: the animal, probably a donkey. Yet that beast was a life-saver. God made him an instrument of one person helping another. He could not be the hero of the story, for he could not voluntarily choose to help the wounded stranger at his own risk and expense. The ability to choose to do God's will is the high dignity of humankind alone. Animals serve God's purposes unknowingly.

We have not only the dignity of free choice, but also the responsibility to use and care for God's creatures rightly and humanely. Animals are to be used for God's glory, in the work of love. That is why God gave us dominion over the beasts of the field and the fruits of the earth.

We can also learn some things from the animals if we have the humility to do so. The patience of the ox, the fidelity of the dog, the courage of the mother wren protecting her offspring, the industry of the bee and the ant: surely God wants us to mark well and to learn. —1960

JULY 12

Matthew 25:10. *Those who were ready went with him into the wedding banquet.*

When I first entered the convent almost fifty years ago, one of our very old sisters died. In those days it was our custom to see the person who had died before the casket was closed and placed in our chapel for a night-long vigil preceding the requiem the next morning. When I looked at Sister Madeline's peaceful, serene face, the faith of her whole life seemed to shine from it. It spoke very powerfully to me. She seemed to be saying: "I was right all along. I gave my life to him because I loved him with all my heart. And he's coming for me now. Thanks be to God!"

The beauty of that radiant sister's face deepened and strengthened my own belief in the Lord I had come to serve. When they say religion is caught not taught, I think I know exactly what they mean. No one ever said in words to me quite so much about the joys of knowing, loving, and serving Christ as Sister Madeline's face did in death. I hope some day to tell her so and thank her.—2006

JULY 13

Matthew 25:21. *Well done, good and faithful slave; you have been trustworthy in a few things, I will put you in charge of many things; enter into the joy of your master.*

A short, heavy man, dressed in a business suit with unpressed trousers was holding the attention of four hundred college students as he talked about Jesus Christ. A square beard did not hide the plainness of his face. Everything about him was subordinate to the impression he made of force, intelligence, and conviction. He was Dwight L. Moody, probably the most powerful Christian of his generation. Many thousands of people learned through him to know and love Jesus Christ.

I remember the thud of Moody's closed fist on the reading desk as he ended his address that night, saying with all the energy that was in him: "I am glad the Lord did not say to anyone: Well done, good and successful servant, but well done, good and faithful servant."

This was one of our Lord's last words on earth. Never mind if you do nothing remarkable for him. He notes your fidelity. Every plodding step you take—one foot before the other—is bringing you into the joy of your Lord.—1944

JULY 14

Matthew 25:40. *Truly I tell you, just as you did it to one of the least of these who are members of my family, you did it to me.*

Mattie and her husband Bert were just passing through town when Bert had a heart attack that left him an invalid. For two years they lived on Social Security in a walk-up flat in a public housing project. Bert died, and the county buried him in a cardboard coffin in the indigent cemetery. Mattie worried about the condition of his grave.

She had a regular visitor from the church and always asked him how Bert's grave looked. Was there grass on it? Neither the county nor the cemetery operators cared about Bert's grave, and outsiders were forbidden to do planting. Early one morning Mattie's friend sneaked into the cemetery with a rake and seed. Soon the grass came, and Mattie was relieved.

That person inspired the founding of the Cup of Cold Water Society. I invite you to join. There are no dues, no officers, no meetings—a thoroughly satisfactory organization. The rules are that when you know someone is in need, maybe for something so simple as a cup of cold water, you help and then tell no one you did it. God will know.—1987

JULY 15

Romans 12:3. *For by the grace given to me I say to everyone among you not to think of yourself more highly than you ought to think.*

An ancient church father said that getting rid of pride was like peeling an onion. You say to yourself, "Now at last pride is gone and the kernel of humility remains." But you find that there is another layer of pride, and another. The outside is gone, but the core is the same.

One place where it clings and is often unrecognized is in our pride of race, class, and nation. Each group tends to believe it is superior to other groups, morally and in the contribution it makes to society and the world. We think we are the people, the hope of civilization, the standard against which others are to be measured. Because there is some truth in this (every group has some virtues), it is difficult to see the subtle role played by pride.

One of the marks of conversion is to follow Saint Paul's advice and not think of ourselves more highly than we ought to. Each race, class, and nation is only one among many, and God wills the existence of us all. Each group under God must play its part while honoring others and the parts they play.—1943

JULY 16

Romans 12:13. *Contribute to the needs of the saints; extend hospitality to strangers.*

Hospitality is a Christian virtue. In Ireland, the level of friendliness toward guests expressed in the greeting of "a hundred thousand welcomes to you" is held to be distinctively Christian. There must be no hard calculation in neighborly love.

Saint Paul, in the latter part of his letter to the Romans, shows how the great doctrines of which he had been writing inspire us to be practical in our Christian living. If God is love, such love must have many shapes and shades in the lives of men and women, the sons and daughters of God.

When there was no room in the inn, the world seemed a friendless place: into its darkness the light of the Son of Man shone. When certain people passed by a poor victim of the roads, a stranger who brought help and gave hospitality interpreted afresh the meaning of the word "neighbor."—1963

JULY 17

Psalm 42:1. *As the deer longs for the water-brooks, so longs my soul for you, O God.*

When Admiral Peary was a boy of ten, he set his heart on discovering the North Pole. All through life he nursed this great desire, no matter how people made fun of him. His response was to dedicate his life toward his goal, and he became the explorer he wanted to be.

When I hear someone say, for instance, "I always wanted to be a teacher," only politeness keeps me from answering, "No, you didn't, or you'd be a teacher. There was no 'always' and you didn't really 'want' it. You just had a little wishfulness now and then."

Let us be honest with ourselves. What do we really want out of life, and want all the time? If we truly long for it, we will work for it, and work for it tirelessly. We will not forget it when something else comes along, and more than likely, it will come to us.

If we want God, if we can say, "As the deer longs for the waterbrooks, so longs my soul for you, O God," we will find God (or God will find us). God may not come to us immediately, but God will come. To want is the first and last essential.—1941

JULY 18

Colossians 1:17. *He himself is before all things, and in him all things hold together.*

An old man was asked the secret of his serenity. He replied, "Son, there's one thing you gotta know. There's only one center to this universe—and you ain't it."

It is hard for us to remember that, for each of us sees the world from his or her own point of view. In that sense each of us is a center of perception, the center of our own little world. And that is what leads to arrogance, misunderstanding, and conflict among us. Only God can be The Center of the universe, of our little worlds and of all the worlds that are. When we discover that Center, it changes profoundly our perception of ourselves, our environment, and other people.

What joy it was for Paul to discover in Jesus Christ a center, not only for his own life but for all life, for all time, and for all things—"the image of the invisible God"—one who reconciled (brought together in a new relationship) the differing and conflicting points of view of Jew and Gentile, man and woman, old and young, those near and those far off. This indeed was a gospel to preach "to every creature under heaven." It still is.—1982

JULY 19

Romans 13:12-14. *The night is far gone, the day is near. Let us then lay aside the works of darkness and put on the armor of light; let us live honorably as in the day, not in reveling and drunkenness, not in debauchery and licentiousness, not in quarreling and jealousy. Instead, put on the Lord Jesus Christ, and make no provision for the flesh, to gratify its desires.*

These were the words that led the great Saint Augustine to Christ. He had been a wayward youth. His mother, Monica, had prayed for him and when she heard about his conversion she said, "My hopes in this world are satisfied."

The old life fell from Augustine as an old garment when he put on the new life in Christ. His life had had no unity. He knew the gospel, yet he lived apart from Christ. He was restless and could not rest till he had found the peace of Christ. Finally, his divided heart found peace. The wall of partition between his false self and his true self had broken down, and Christ now filled Augustine's entire life. We hear him saying, "I could not exist, therefore my God, were it not for your existence in me."

As for Augustine, so for us.—1948

JULY 20

Mark 7:6. *[Jesus] said to them, "Isaiah prophesied rightly about you hypocrites, as it is written, 'This people honors me with their lips, but their hearts are far from me.'"*

Sometimes I wonder if the church really is making progress on our journey to the kingdom. Are we making a difference? Do we worship in vain? Like the hypocrites?

Our bishop made his annual visitation to our parish. There was much preparation and excitement. On the morning of the big day, worship began with a grand procession. When the bishop arrived at the chair of honor, he found one of our newest acolytes sitting in it.

She was maybe ten years old. "Young lady," he asked, "Do you know where you are sitting?" "Oh yes, sir," she responded, "I sit here every Sunday." He graciously moved to the seat next to her. Later in the day, he commended her good service.

I know that we so often don't get it right and only see in a mirror dimly. That Sunday our bishop showed us all that the kingdom really is at hand and that the church—often in unexpected ways—can even show us the way to that kingdom. You can reach out and touch it—and sometimes even sit down right next to it.—2013

JULY 21

Psalm 119:71. *It is good for me that I have been afflicted, that I might learn your statutes.*

Why is it that when we are "down with the fish" (a favorite saying of a dear friend), we dig ourselves deeper into that dark place in our lives and only in retrospect see God's presence? I have been lost, confused, at the end of my rope, and unable to see anything but afflictions in my life—divorce, shattered hopes and dreams, fears for myself and my children. Is this not true for all of us? It is in that time of affliction that I have turned to God, felt God's grace, and grown from those experiences.

With God's grace and spiritual friends who walked with me and talked with me, I can look back on those times and say, as the psalmist said, "It is good for me that I have been afflicted" because I came to a place to say, "God, I need your help."

I had to move from that place of knowing about God to that place of knowing God. This move was from my head to my heart—trusting that the unknown would become clear, as I trusted in God's presence. Today, God is in the midst of my life. I know in my heart that God's comfort is always greater than any affliction and when my faith falters, as it will do, I can hold onto that hopeful promise given in his Word.—2003

JULY 22

Romans 12:3. *For by the grace given to me I say to everyone among you not to think of yourself more highly than you ought to think, but to think with sober judgment, each according to the measure of faith that God has assigned.*

I'm not much, but I'm all I think about.

So many decisions each day and most, if not all, of them are centered around self. Each of us has a set of scales—many sets in fact—constantly weighing the pros and cons of every behavior. How will this help? How will this hurt?

A certain degree of this is helpful. For instance, it is wise to not walk across a busy street without looking. However, the instinct to protect self can run amok. Suddenly, protection of self becomes promotion of self. Erroneously, we fear no one else is going to speak up for us, so if we want to be heard or recognized, we better blow our own horn. Either that or, deep down, the way we see ourselves is so distorted that we seek to bolster our perception with self-service.

Seeing ourselves as right-sized can be a lifetime process for some. Finally settling in, we find it fits like nothing else.—2014

JULY 23

Psalm 51:11. *Create in me a clean heart, O God.*

Stuart Chase tells of a brilliant young accountant who, after earning his C.P.A., had an opportunity to make a million dollars in a few weeks' time by certain questionable methods. The methods had to do with adjusting income tax returns. He told his mother of the glittering opportunity which had been offered him.

"Tom," she said, "you know when I come to wake you up in the morning, I shake you hard, and you don't stir." "Yes," he replied. "And then I shake you harder and you give a little moan." "Yes," he replied again. "And finally I shake as hard as I can, and you open one sleepy eye." "Yes," came the reply the third time. "Well," said his mother, "I'd hate to come into your room morning after morning and find you wide awake." The young man turned down the job.

Bookstores today devote entire shelves to advice about ways to reduce tension, prevent strain and worry, and gain that precious possession known as peace of mind. The source of the most profound inner peace and serenity is not anything recently discovered. It is a clean heart before God, the habit of inner integrity, a clear conscience. —1965

🕮🕮

JULY 24

Matthew 27:21. *The governor again said to them, "Which of the two do you want me to release for you?" And they said, "Barabbas."*

On television there was a special about the vault under the headquarters of Prohibition era gangster Al Capone, a man who made a vast fortune suborning, threatening, bribing, murdering, and generally thumbing his nose at laws and mores. As men and machines dug through walls for the hidden treasure, survivors of Capone's heyday remembered him. Most looked back nostalgically, remembering the "good times" and how great they had felt in the presence of such an important man.

There is something in us that wants to make heroes of terrible people. Jesse James, Bonnie and Clyde—Robin Hoods? Hitler and Mussolini—geniuses, saviors? For a while, it may seem.

And so the crowd called for Pilate to let Barabbas go free and to crucify Jesus. However we explain it— fallenness, original sin, animal nature—there is something awfully wrong with us, demonstrated by the company we seek.

Incidentally, Capone's vault turned out to be empty. But then, it always had been.—1987

JULY 25

Luke 11:13. *If you then, who are evil, know how to give good gifts to your children, how much more will the heavenly Father give the Holy Spirit to those who ask him!*

You want your child to "ask…seek…knock" when he comes to you. So, says Jesus, does your Father in heaven. Moreover, you want your child to spell out plainly to you what he wants. But do you not, sometimes, sit down with him to talk it over and ask if he really wants this or only thinks he does?

Of course you want to give good gifts to your child, but what is the good gift? He wants to play ball when you want him to do his arithmetic. Which will be the "good gift"—your permission to skip the homework and play ball, or your insistence that he do the lesson first?

This can be a problem for us, but it is never a problem for God. God doesn't need to debate with himself what the good gift is. When he sends it to you—whatever it is—it is the good gift.—1960

JULY 26

Matthew 20:25-27. *You know that the rulers of the Gentiles lord it over them, and their great ones are tyrants over them. It will not be so among you; but whoever wishes to be great among you must be your servant, and whoever wishes to be first among you must be your slave.*

If Christianity is to win the world, Christians must unite upon certain fundamental objectives and seek to discover practical means for their attainment.

One is the elimination of war.

A second is a social order which gives to able and competent human beings the opportunity to work and earn a living wage.

A third is the elimination of the selfish exploitation by the strong of the weaker members of society.

Not only must we make Christianity more vital and telling by strengthening our own faith and by translating our faith into action, but also each separate individual follower of Christ must learn to live in closer comradeship with him. This will mean assuming the form of servant, letting go of our own prerogatives and claims. Our love of Christ makes this possible. It is only as we come to know and love Christ passionately that we can through our lives make his spirit irradiate this dark world.—1941

⚜⚜

JULY 27

Psalm 61:1-2. *Hear my cry, O God, and listen to my prayer. I call upon you from the ends of the earth with heaviness in my heart; set me upon the rock that is higher than I.*

A few years ago, after spending several days in an emotional sinking spell, I shared with a close friend my dark mood.

"Do you pray every day?" he asked gently.

"Of course!" I snapped.

"What do you pray?" he persisted.

My prayers sounded much like this psalmist's lament: "Hear my cry, God, and respond soon, for my heart is overwhelmed."

My friend smiled. "And when do you start this prayer?" he questioned.

"As soon as I feel depressed."

My friend suggested a different strategy, one I still use: "The moment you awake, before you even get out of bed, think of ten things about your life which are good and promising, or at least less discouraging than before. Thank God for each of these."

My friend was telling me to choose deliberately the way I would begin each day, and to begin with a spirit of thanksgiving. Try it. You'll like it.—1992

JULY 28

Acts 1:11. *Men of Galilee, why do you stand looking up toward heaven? This Jesus, who has been taken up from you into heaven, will come in the same way as you saw him go into heaven.*

Atomic fission makes the world's end very real. It should sober us all to work and sacrifice for peace. We could destroy the world—world suicide—but we dare not say that thereby we could force the Lord's Second Coming.

The gospel tells of the world's end, but in dramatic symbolism. Christ will take charge in a fitting climax to the drama of creation. The point is not a great explosion, but that "this Jesus" will come to us as he came to the disciples whose experience we long for.

Many early Christians were paralyzed by expecting the Lord's immediate Second Coming.

You know how it is when you wait for a train which "will be here any minute." What use is it to do anything? Saint Paul, revising his own first belief, had to tell the churches in Thessalonica that the time of the Lord's return was not to be on their minds. Let them serve him who indeed might come anytime, but study to be serene and do your own business.—1948

JULY 29

Matthew 27:63. *"After three days I will rise again."*

Jesus was crucified, his body laid in the tomb, but still the Jewish leaders asked Pilate to seal the sepulchre so that the body of Jesus could not be carried away and the disciples mislead the people.

Ever since, people have tried to lock up Christ lest he upset the state of things as they are. They have asked his disciples not to preach, for fear they might carry further the disturbance Jesus had begun.

Yet people cannot seal off the spirit of Christ. There is no human-made tomb strong enough to contain him. The history of the Christian centuries has shown the explosive power of the resurrection. The risen Christ broke through the shackles of the Roman Empire and in four centuries it was in ruins. When people tried to confine him in the thought forms of the Middle Ages, he broke through once more in the Reformation.

Today the spirit of Christ is bursting the sepulchre once again. Wherever Christians bring their faith to bear on the political, economic, and social tensions of the day, the stone is rolled away and Christ lives again, often surprising even those who bear his name. Let us not join the obscurantists who in every age have tried to seal the tomb and confine Christ there.—1971

❧❦❧❦

JULY 30

Acts 2:12-13. *All were amazed and perplexed, saying to one another, "What does this mean?" But others sneered and said, "They are filled with new wine."*

I do a lot of pre-marriage counseling, and I thoroughly enjoy it. Newly engaged couples are wonderful to be around. They are so totally involved with one another, and they are hopelessly excited about the possibilities of their future together.

The challenge of this counseling is to try to help the couple ask the right questions of themselves and each other to insure they can build a good foundation for a solid marriage. I always approach the task remembering the words of Robert Runcie, the former archbishop of Canterbury, who observed that "...marriage is the only life-long covenant the church asks a couple to make while they are in a state of temporary insanity."

On the Day of Pentecost the disciples, filled with the Holy Spirit, were thought to be either drunk or insane. They were neither, but they were love-struck—filled with the empowering love of God.

People in love sometimes do foolish things. They behave in wonderfully odd ways. Saint Paul bids us to be "fools for Christ"— love-struck for him and his world.—1996

JULY 31

Matthew 28:20. *And remember, I am with you always, to the end of the age.*

To the ends of the earth and to the end of time, Jesus assures us he will never abandon us. He says to us, "You will never find yourself where I have not gone before, or without guidance, if you turn to me. I who am the Way will prepare the way for my witnesses. I who am the Truth will be there to help when the right words do not come easily or the right decision seems unclear. I who am the Life will revive you when energies dwindle and hope fades. And at the end, I who have been with you all along, the Alpha and the Omega, will embrace you as my own." Blessed assurance.

The trouble is, it does not always seem that way. We know dark nights of the soul that may go on for months. We can name God-forsaken places, not all of them at the ends of the earth. We struggle with doubt, defeat, and ineffectiveness. The words of faith seem so easy for others that we cannot believe they have faced the tough questions.

Jesus did not say he would spare us this, but that even when we doubt his presence, he will be there.—1984

AUGUST

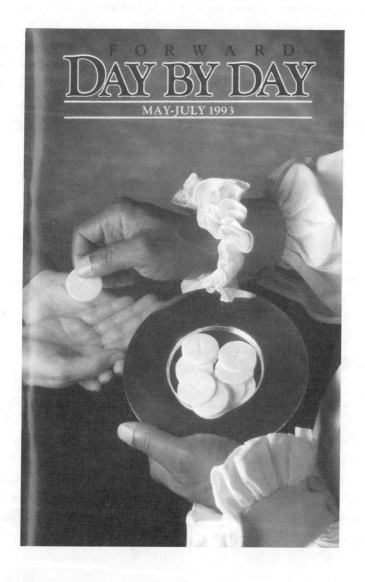

AUGUST 1

Mark 12:31. *There is no other commandment greater than these.*

My confirmation teacher was one tough cookie. Two days before the bishop's visitation, I was still on the hook for some memory work and written assignments. Late in the afternoon, my teacher stopped by our home for the final examination. She looked at everything and tested me on my memory work. It all looked good, and my mother breathed a huge sigh of relief.

And then my teacher said, "One more question." My heart sank. "Tell me Jesus' summary of the law." Well, I had that one down and zipped right through it. And then she came in with a follow-up. "Why do you think it is important?" My response was tentative, something along the lines of, "If I obey the commandment, some day after I die, I will be allowed to get into the kingdom?"

She smiled and said, "Close, but a little off." Then she explained that Jesus gave us the summary of the law so we could get into the kingdom right now. "Live the commandment," she said, "and live in the kingdom."

I have pretty much forgotten the assignments I had to complete for confirmation class, but I will always remember what my teacher taught me on the last day.—2013

AUGUST 2

John 1:18. *No one has ever seen God.*

No one has seen or can see all of God at any one time. We do see a part of God made manifest each day. It is almost as if each night we die and then God touches us and restores us to life each morning. God is nearer than hands and feet. Indeed God is both hands and feet—and brain and eyes and beating heart. That is why it is possible to feel God's presence and to hear and see God's moments of illuminating light and directing love.

That is why we need to stay so close to Jesus. Jesus allowed God's will to control his life. God's kingdom began in Jesus. He was the first pioneer of the kingdom, for the kingdom begins when a person is obedient to God. More than once he said that the kingdom was here among us, that it was beginning to germinate within us. The kingdom is among us today. Whenever and wherever men and women turn to God, the kingdom comes and new cells of life begin to grow.—1977

AUGUST 3

Acts 3:6. *Peter said, "I have no silver or gold, but what I have I give you; in the name of Jesus Christ of Nazareth, stand up and walk."*

We are healed by going.

"Go and show yourselves to the priests," Jesus told the ten lepers. "Go and do likewise" ended the parable of the Good Samaritan. "Go forth in peace." Such was the apostolic benediction. Members of Alcoholics Anonymous realize that the principle of going is essential in healing.

The mission of the Christian is to go forth in Christ's name. When do you plan to take off? Begin in your home, Jerusalem, and then with your neighbors, Samaria, before you serve in the uttermost parts. Discouraging at first? Of course! How few people share our Lord's wisdom! We will not succeed in every venture; all people may not be able to pay the cost of discipleship. Only from time to time will we be privileged to observe success; ventures started by us are often completed by others.

Discipleship begins by knowing Jesus, develops by showing him, and is fulfilled by going forth. With his courage replacing our timidity, we can demonstrate to others a higher level of life. We have a story to tell. What a tragedy if we should fail to tell it.—1972

AUGUST 4

John 1:40-42. *One of the two who heard John speak and followed him was Andrew, Simon Peter's brother. He first found his brother Simon and said to him, "We have found the Messiah" (which is translated Anointed). He brought Simon to Jesus.*

If Jesus came along, what would you do? Would you ask favors of him, blow your own horn, flatter him? Or would you find your brother and bring him to Jesus?

Whatever Andrew might have done, his greatness lay in what he did do. He went and found his brother and brought him to Jesus.

The experience of centuries of growth of the church has confirmed the fact that while services, evangelistic meetings, broadcasts, and innumerable other things may convert people to Christ, no outreach can take the place of Andrew's method of the personal invitation.

How different Christian history would have been had Andrew not brought Peter to Jesus! No matter what else Andrew did in his whole life, the most valuable contribution he made to Christianity was to find his brother.

It is easy to speak to someone you scarcely know, but difficult to talk to those who are most aware of your own failings. But you aren't failing here if you bring another to the One who never fails. Have I ever won anyone for Jesus? How hard have I tried?—1943

❦❧

AUGUST 5

Psalm 145:17. *You open wide your hand and satisfy the needs of every living creature.*

Do you say grace before meals in your family?

The use of a grace is at once an act of thanksgiving and an act of humility. The grace reminds us that God is the Giver and that we are dependent upon God for life itself. The use of a grace can also serve to bring peace and quietness to restless children and tired parents. There are a number of familiar graces that members of the family may learn and use. Here is one by poet Richard Euringer that I have just discovered and like particularly for its biblical allusions and its poetry: O Thou who clothest the lilies, And feedest the birds of the sky, Who leadest the lambs to the pasture, And the hart to the waterside, Who hast multiplied the loaves and fishes, And converted water into wine; Do Thou come to our table As Guest and Giver to dine.

The Sermon on the Mount, Psalms 23 and 42, the feeding of the five thousand, the marriage feast in Cana, and the Lord's Supper are all suggested in this gracious blessing. It helps us to remember that Jesus still comes to nourish and strengthen us with his most holy presence.—1953

AUGUST 6

Luke 9:33. *Peter said to Jesus, "Master, it is good for us to be here."*

Like Peter, James, and John, we too have our "mountaintop moments," and the glory of them often stays with us to sustain us when the going gets rough. For some it may be church-related, the memory of their first communion, the breathless hush of the early-morning stillness broken only by the warm, wonderful words of worship. For others it may be some spectacle of nature, perhaps a summer sunset, or the snow-capped Tetons, perfectly reflected in the mirror of Jackson Lake. For still others it may be the moment they first understood, with a flash of almost divine intuition, the meaning of love. So we garden-variety mortals are given our lesser transfigurations, those glimpses of unearthly beauty when we know with a certainty beyond all argument that we stand in the presence of something infinitely greater than ourselves.

Like the apostles, we also must descend again into the valley of dull, daily routine, the valley of decision where choices must be made and their results lived with, even the valley of the shadow of death. Jesus came down from the mountain with the apostles, and he walks in the valley with us.—1978

AUGUST 7

John 2:24-25. *But Jesus on his part would not entrust himself to them, because he knew all people and needed no one to testify about anyone; for he himself knew what was in everyone.*

How deep is the pain when someone we admire is caught in a disgraceful sin or betrayal! How great is the shock when we sin in some way we'd never imagined we could. Disillusionment, rage, defeat, and hopelessness may swirl around us. How can I forgive them, how can I forgive myself? Some of the emotional storm comes simply from our naïveté.

With God there is no naïveté. Jesus displays penetrating insight as he looks at Peter and Judas and John and Mary Magdalene and the rich young ruler. He reaches out to them, he gives his life for them, not because he is an untutored optimist but because he knows the possibilities of both good and evil in God's world. Unlikely ones respond, like tax-collectors and centurions. Peter can flounder around, a hero today and a flop tomorrow. Each of us is an astounding mixture of promise and betrayal; he knows and seeks us anyway. Jesus does not shrink from Judas; it is Judas who gives up on Jesus.—1990

AUGUST 8

Luke 12:34. *For where your treasure is, there your heart will be also.*

What do we value most highly in our lives, not just in fine principle but in daily practice? Our creature comforts, or our immortal souls? Our morning prayers, or that first cup of coffee? Before saying "My prayers, of course!" look again. Confronted by a choice between spending this evening with a lonely soul in a rest home or relaxing in front of the television for your favorite program, which do you want to do? Where is your treasure? For there your heart, your enthusiasm, your pleasure, will be.

We all need an occasional audit and overhaul of our hearts' treasures. If you are the sole exception, blessed are you. Do write a book and tell us how you do it. It will be a best seller.—1964

❧❧❧

AUGUST 9

John 3:4. *Nicodemus said to him, "How can anyone be born after having grown old?"*

Is it possible for you and me to be transformed for the better? Can we observe change? If you spend any time serving the needs of people, and especially needy persons, persons with chronic problems, you develop a sort of reticence, even pessimism about their ability to change.

The Lord envisioned character change. As with most changes in society, change is created through the unasked-for devastation of loss and rejection.

One way of saying this is that people never change and people can always change. Both sides are true. I am like a block of steel most of the time—my flaws and givens are stiff and solid. But crisis and tragedy can change the steel to jelly, and I become as pliable as a living thing could possibly be.

We are set in concrete as the result of our psycho-genetic inwardness which scripture names sin. At the same time, we are soft and churning soil waiting for the seed of love to be planted and to create a copious tree, shading the world and lending strength to the weak.—1993

AUGUST 10

John 3:30. *He must increase, but I must decrease.*

John the Baptist was the forerunner, the one who pointed out Jesus as the Lamb of God and testified to the vision of the Holy Spirit anointing him at the time of his baptism. This was the beginning of Jesus' mission. Two of John's disciples followed Jesus.

Others remained with John, and now they experience a common human reaction in the face of change. They hurt to see large numbers flocking to Jesus while John's following is shrinking. "All are going to him," they say.

But John is content. He knows that he has fulfilled his mission. He bore faithful witness to the One who was to come and baptize with the Holy Spirit. In the increase of the followers of Jesus, John sees his own success. Like the best man at the wedding, waiting for the bridegroom to arrive, he can only rejoice on hearing the bridegroom's voice.

The sense of frustration in John's followers is understandable. It is very much like our own when we have labored devotedly to build up our church, only to find that a new generation is taking over. John reassures us. The one taking over, in the guise of newcomers and strangers, is none other than Jesus himself.—1978

AUGUST 11

John 4:4. *But he had to go through Samaria.*

Our meditation is moving into a great story in John's Gospel, and we pause to look at this very human detail: "He had to go through Samaria." This was in the course of Jesus' journey from Judea to Galilee. Passing through Samaria was a distasteful experience for a Jew, and one that could be dangerous, for there was bad blood between Jews and Samaritans. What this tells us is that when the Son of God was made flesh and dwelt among us, he did not so choose his human company and his geographical habitat that he would never come into contact with people who were not of his sort. He was a Jew; he could not pass through Samaria without experiencing the hostility of most Samaritans and the hatred of some.

What did Jesus do as he faced this ever so human problem? He didn't make a wide detour of the place where these human undesirables lived. There was voluntary, mutual segregation between Jew and Samaritan. Instead, he simply cut across that line. If "Samaria"—symbolizing the unpleasant people we don't want to deal with face-to-face—stood in his path, he walked calmly through it rather than around it. And he met somebody there whom he regarded as abundantly worth meeting. That just could happen to us.—1970

AUGUST 12

Psalm 105:1. *Give thanks to the LORD and call upon his Name; make known his deeds among the peoples.*

A school bus went off a mountain road. In the crash, the driver and many children died. Others were seriously injured. Amidst the grief, terror, and lawsuits, parents eventually asked "Where is God? How can we ever live with thanksgiving again? How can we ever believe that God is good?"

God gives us two responses to those questions. God is present everywhere; he is in the bus, as he was on the cross. God suffers and dies with us. God is in the hospital room, workplace, battlefield, courtroom, prison cell, and on the cross. Also, God is in the stirrings of new life—in the outreached hand, the breath of compassion, the wailing that turns into a hymn.

The psalms urge us to cry out, mourn, and call for help. Present to us, God hears our cry. In the comfort of the Holy Spirit are the stirrings of new life. The Lord's mercy endures forever.—1993

AUGUST 13

Psalm 107:2. *Let all those whom the Lord has redeemed proclaim that he redeemed them from the hand of the foe.*

Several mornings in a row I woke up with a headache. My job was very distasteful then. Conversation and adapting myself to people seemed impossible. I would have given anything to be able to avoid living those days.

Then it dawned on me that if my doings had no significance, God's had. He was trying to make the world a better place that day. He was trying to get people to live together in friendship. If I could take some part in his work, then my life would be worthwhile. It might be difficult to meet people in Christ's spirit of friendship and to do the details of my work carefully when my head felt as though an engine were throbbing inside it. But all that was of small importance if by that effort I could fit into God's great task and be an agent through whom some of his love could flow to people.

My perspective changed. I began to see not my difficulties, but the onward march of God's purpose. In that I could exult with the psalmist, "They cried to the Lord in their trouble, and he delivered them from their distress."—1947

AUGUST 14

Psalm 107:33-37. *The Lord changed rivers into deserts, and water-springs into thirsty ground, a fruitful land into salt flats, because of the wickedness of those who dwell there. He changed deserts into pools of water and dry land into water-springs. He settled the hungry there, and they founded a city to dwell in. They sowed fields, and planted vineyards, and brought in a fruitful harvest.*

In this psalm God is shown at work, guiding and helping people in ordinary life. The normal unfailing care of God for us all is vividly brought before us to awaken our wonder and gratitude. Growing seed feeds the hungry, travelers are guided on their way, ships are led though the perils of the sea, lands are irrigated and made productive, cities are built and governed, penitents are forgiven. Each picture ends with an exhortation to praise.

Times of great deliverance move us to thanksgiving, but we are apt to take daily blessings for granted. Do we have the habit of seeing God in everything and giving thanks? This psalmist even sees God at work when the springs dry up and the crops fail. A thankful spirit sees more and more things for which to be thankful.—1939

AUGUST 15

Hebrews 12:1. *We are surrounded by so great a cloud of witnesses.*

My mother died at the age of ninety-five. After her death I was told that I had thirty days to clear out her apartment. It was agonizing. A whole part of my life seemed to be disappearing as her belongings left.

On the last day, I decided to return to the apartment for one last look at the empty space. Just as I turned to leave, my eye caught a piece of paper on the floor beside the place where her bed had been. I reached to pick it up and discovered much to my astonishment that it was a beautifully printed prayer card which she had treasured, with the words of the Lord's Prayer.

I stood there in disbelief. And suddenly it was clear. I became aware that she was with me and would always be. She was part of the cloud of witnesses of whom the author of Hebrews speaks. She had witnessed to the substance of love, which is endless and eternal. The church without this dimension of heavenly witness is really not the church. That prayer card now sits on my desk to remind me always of that fact.—2004

AUGUST 16

Psalm 34:8. *Taste and see that the LORD is good.*

On a retreat, we were given a small pocket notebook titled "Senses Census." The retreat leader then sent us out on a walk to collect and record what we saw, heard, felt, smelled, and tasted.

As I crunched over the gravel walkway leading to the trail, I heard a meadowlark singing and felt the wind against my cheek. The taste of the lunch dessert, a fresh lemon meringue pie, lingered in my mouth. Blooming cactus complemented the smell of sage, as did the sound of thunder with the darkening skies overhead. Workers chattered and laughed, listening to radio music as they put stucco on a house. An American flag fluttered on a pole. I visually explored the undulating red rock formations of the Colorado National Monument that stretched across the horizon, and stood for a long while watching the light changing across its surfaces. In the distance, I heard a bell ringing, indicating it was time to come back in and share our census with the other retreatants.

The psalmist suggests that we can know God through our senses—and not only that we can know God, but we can know that God is good.—2006

❧❧❧

AUGUST 17

Psalm 121:1-2. *From where is my help to come? My help comes from the LORD.*

We spend a lot of time planning for security in our later years. A comfortable retirement appeals to us. Even more, we don't want to be dependent on our children or the government.

Living in a retirement community, I see around me the varied results of those plans. Some people are doing well, while others have had a sudden stroke, debilitating disease, or serious accident, and their secure base is melting away. Most of us are independent, but some must rely on assisted living. A few, some with dementia, live on for decades. There is little we can do about it. The fact is, God is our only security. The Lord's promises don't fail us, even when they are not what we expect. Those of us in our eighties have lived through calamities and wars. We know the uncertainty of "best-laid-plans." A prayer of Thomas Merton puts it this way: "You will lead me by the right road though I may know nothing about it. Therefore will I trust you always…I will not fear, for…you will never leave me to face my perils alone."

The ability to love as Jesus loved is beyond all of us. But I believe God will indeed lead us in the right way when we ask. And we can trust him. Always.—2005

☙☙☙

AUGUST 18

1 Timothy 6:6-7. *There is great gain in godliness combined with contentment; for we brought nothing into the world, so that we can take nothing out of it.*

Contentment is our deep heart's craving. But it seems to flicker on the razor's edge of the present, and then it's gone. Think of the strategies we've created to lure contentment in and make it stay. All of us have tried to build contentment on the scaffolding of pleasant circumstances—a good meal, the next vacation at some Walden Pond, anything to banish anxiety and apprehension. But that sort of contentment can be ripped away with the next phone call.

Another strategy is to protect our hearts by expecting less, turning down the dimmer switch on hope. ("Christmas is never as wonderful for the grownups as for the kids," we say, numb to the expansive wonder of the Incarnation.) It is a form of Christian stoicism yielding less pain, but no joy, no contentment.

Where do we go to find contentment? Psalm 131 pictures a contentment nothing in this world brings: "I still my soul and make it quiet, like a child upon its mother's breast; my soul is quieted within me. O, Israel, wait upon the LORD from this time forth for evermore." —2012

AUGUST 19

John 6:27. *Do not work for the food that perishes, but for the food that endures for eternal life, which the Son of Man will give you.*

Jimmy Novak was a former sailor living on the lower East Side of New York City. We met at the soup kitchen run by the parish of Holy Apostles. It was the soup kitchen's fifteenth anniversary. I was assigned to write about Manhattan's largest feeding program. More than 1,200 people would be fed that day. "I look around this room and say to myself, 'There but for the grace of God go I,'" Jimmy said.

"I stood in bread and soup lines during the Depression. I always said, 'I only hope that some day I can pay this back.' I don't have a lot of money, and I could never afford to pay back what I was given, but I do have time, and time is what I give."

"What does this mean to you?" I asked.

Jimmy glared at me. He turned toward the bustling room and said: "I believe in God. I come to church. I come back because I have no other place to go. But I love the people. I come here to feed them. Go tell that story." He put his coat on and walked away.

This man, with all of his miseries and joys, had just summed up the entire gospel message. Love God. Love each other. Feed my sheep. Go tell the world.—2002

AUGUST 20

John 6:35. *Jesus said to them, "I am the bread of life. Whoever comes to me will never be hungry, and whoever believes in me will never be thirsty."*

In one of the most profound yet simply stated sayings of the whole of the New Testament, Jesus says, "I am the bread of life." A few paragraphs cannot come close to interpreting the many facets of this famous verse. It is at the same time eucharistic, a metaphor about faith, and a program for living in the present, but with implications for eternal life.

In the eucharist we symbolically partake of bread, the most basic food there is, thus indicating all sustenance, which is created by God who is the source of all sustenance. As a faith statement, we "come to" him and "believe in" him, thus satisfying our wanderlust for the truth and our search for someone to trust.

The promise of life is contained in this simple statement, but it is not merely plain living that is meant, but the abundant life (John 10:10). When this gospel mentions "life," it usually means this life and the life to come as one continuum. And so it is here. He will give us life, sustain our life, stretch our life, so that nothing shall be lost. He promises to do this now. He will do this by raising us up to be with him at the appropriate day.—1981

AUGUST 21

Hebrews 13:5. *Keep your lives free from the love of money, and be content with what you have. "*

We found some people who were in deep financial trouble and had to get rid of their boat. We got it for practically nothing!"

It was a bargain. It was sharp dealing. But was it right? To look for and find someone on whose misfortune one could capitalize? Greed may be the most insidious of sins because it is so accepted. Hasn't everyone done just exactly what this family did, for a house, a car, a bicycle? Much of our lives are spent pursuing bargains, something for nothing.

Many people have the same attitude about their spiritual lives: Get as much as possible for as little as possible. God, the church, and Christianity are supposed to meet all their spiritual needs at bargain prices. There are religion shoppers, too. And there are those who think God is so desperate for souls that he will surely lower the requirements at the last moment. But as far as we know, there are no bargain days in heaven and God is not desperate.

Lord, I don't want a bargain. I want you.—1973

AUGUST 22

Jeremiah 1:7. *But the Lord said to me, "Do not say, 'I am only a boy.'"*

"I'm only a..." How many times have we heard these words, or spoken them? It is one of the most familiar, and oldest, excuses on record. God asks Jeremiah to begin his prophetic ministry while he is still a young man, but I suspect it is not just his youth that prompts his response.

Most of us fulfill ordinary tasks with confidence, but when asked to make a public witness of our faith, our almost knee-jerk reaction is to pull back. "Let someone else do it. He or she is more worthy, more skilled, holier." Yet throughout scripture there are many examples of God choosing the most unlikely candidates. There is no point to telling God about our unworthiness. God created us and knows the number of hairs on our heads. We need only agree to play our part; God does the rest.

Even as I write this, I am pulling out the "only" excuse. "Lord, I am only a sinner. I am only a seeker. What could I possibly have to say that would be of any value?" The answer is clear: we must begin each day not by looking at our deficiencies, but by holding in our hearts God's call to be an active, faith-filled community.—1998

AUGUST 23

John 6:58. *This is the bread that came down from heaven...The one who eats this bread will live forever.*

In making hospital rounds I once visited a lady and asked if she would like to receive Holy Communion. For three Mondays her answer was the same: "Oh, I don't feel very well in the mornings, so I guess I'll just skip it today." Finally, I suggested that Holy Communion might be just what she needed to make her feel better all the time. She looked at me as though such a thing had never occurred to her. The hospital is not the place for sermons, so let me tell you what I would like to have said to her.

The Blessed Sacrament is not like hot cereal or a dessert that one decides to "just skip" today. This is the bread of life! Millions can attest to the healing love, strength, and grace that have come into their bodies, minds, and souls through this very bread. Don't we believe Jesus? Don't we believe what as a sacramental church we have always professed? If anyone eats Christ's Body and drinks his Blood, that person lives forever. How tragic that when Jesus offers himself for us in our greatest need, we should reject him. Let it not be so among you.—1971

❧❧❧

AUGUST 24

Luke 22:24. *A dispute also arose among them as to which one of them was to be regarded as the greatest.*

Francis of Assisi sought obscurity and found greatness. Many other people who sought no fame are remembered centuries later, while the important and notable people of their day—the people in high position and high regard—are long forgotten.

All of us have our greatness in God. This is what the disciples in their dispute over who was greatest did not realize. In the sight of God they had a greatness which they needed only to accept and in which they could find joy.

The same is true for us. We may burn ourselves out trying to achieve greatness or status. We may be unhappy because others hold positions of great importance and we do not. We may be filled with envy and jealousy or bitterness because we have not achieved our hopes and goals. We can take heart because we have our greatness in God—in that we can rejoice. We are God's children, and nothing can take that away from us.—1981

AUGUST 25

Acts 10:4. *"Your prayers and your alms have ascended as a memorial before God."*

How can our prayer become effectual? If our prayers are merely words directed at God, they are—well, merely words.

What we pray for must first be already begun in ourselves. If we would pray for peace, we must already be peacemakers. If we would have forgiveness, we must already be forgiving.

Some are so advanced as to pray for their enemies. To make this effectual we must first consider: has my enemy something against me? Am I willing to amend that offense of mine so that we may be reconciled? It is no use to pray for our enemies if we are looking down upon them.

Our actions must be in line with our prayers. It would baffle anyone—even God—to hear someone say, "I am coming toward you" who all the while was walking in the opposite direction. "Your prayers and your alms have ascended as a memorial before God."
—1940

AUGUST 26

John 7:15. *How does this man have such learning, when he has never been taught?*

It wasn't true that Jesus had never been taught. He would have known the Hebrew scriptures well and have been able to recite long passages of them from memory. But he was not a professional teacher within the established structures of Judaism. Aspiring rabbis developed their reputations as scholars through discipleship with eminent teachers, establishing their own authority on the basis of the authority of their masters. People would tell stories of this or that contest between two famous rabbis and argue about which one's argument was the soundest, somewhat as people today argue about the relative merits of baseball players. These stories of famous rabbis are still told among Jewish scholars. What puzzles his hearers in today's reading: Jesus is acting like a rabbi but lacks the appropriate credentials and pedigree.

God often surprises us that way. Jesus' consistent preference for people on the fringes of society—fishermen, tax collectors—is one such surprise. So was his humble birth. The people we encounter who unexpectedly teach us something about God's love are not always religious professionals in religious settings. God sprinkles them throughout the world, and we happen upon them.—1994

❧❧❧

AUGUST 27

John 8:32. *You will know the truth, and the truth will make you free.*

The truth has not always made me free. The truth of learning that a loved one has been terribly injured or has contracted an incurable disease, or that one has lost his or her job hurts me as I grieve the capriciousness of life.

Things break. People die. As Leonard Cohen sings about suffering, "There is a crack in everything. That's how the light gets in." The truth cracks us.

But there is a larger truth waiting behind the curtain of human drama, and that is the resurrection. Yes, we all die. Even the Son of God was lifted up on the cross and died. But that cross is also where God gathers in every truth and every misery of our lives and administers a higher truth: resurrection. We are born again and set free.

Give thanks today for the things that are cracked and broken in your life. Those are the places where resurrection and new life will occur.—2006

AUGUST 28

John 8:16. *Yet even if I do judge, my judgment would be valid.*

The real barrier to our welcoming of Jesus Christ is not a sophisticated mind but an unworthy life. Sin is often the obstacle; there are things in our lives which we will have to abandon if Christ comes in. That is why the world rejects him. If he came in, the war and greed in our lives, and many a social evil they have produced, would have to go. So he is still despised and rejected of men.

You, too, may be saying—perhaps not out loud but in your heart—"There is no room, no room at all." If someone says that with vehement determination, barring the door against Christ and choosing to live with company that would have to leave were Christ to enter, how can a preacher's words melt that deliberate refusal?

But if some are saying "no room" humbly, because their lives seem too soiled to welcome so great a guest, then there is hope. He did not come at first to a palace, but to a stable, and through the centuries since he never has despised the common, vulgar, and soiled dwelling places. Such are his ways. He seeks us out wherever and however we are living our lives. And what amazing consequence has come to those who have welcomed him!—1977

AUGUST 29

Ephesians 2:7. *So that in the ages to come he might show the immeasurable riches of his grace in kindness toward us in Christ Jesus.*

Just how much are "immeasurable riches"? The riches referred to here are God's riches, which he shares "in kindness toward us in Christ Jesus." Later on in this epistle Paul tells us to "be imitators of God." Sharing of riches is a choice God makes; some of us do not. Something needs to happen to loosen up the hold, to inspire sharing.

Why do so many of our children live in poverty when others nearby live so comfortably? Imagine you are a child in that situation.

The Pine Ridge Reservation in South Dakota is located in several of the poorest counties in the United States. Children do not eat. They are not educated. They are often exposed to violence that results from being totally disempowered. Many children fall victim to suicide.

There are immeasurable riches in the United States. We are all impacted by how they are shared. Our personal tithe of our own wealth is a great step in beginning to address the needs of the whole Christian family.—2012

❧❧❧❧

AUGUST 30

Psalm 39:4. *While I pondered, the fire burst into flame.*

"Activism does not make theologians…The voice of God is heard only in quiet. Good tidings are at everyone's door if they would stop talking and listen to the knock."

These are the words of Archbishop Fulton J. Sheen, advice from a wise priest that every Christian should take seriously. He calls it the "therapy of silence." It is true that the more burdened we are with responsibilities, the more we need silence to meditate.

It is in meeting God in this quietness, alone, that we begin to learn how to hear God's voice. It is in meeting God face to face that we are brought to see our sinfulness and to know forgiveness. It is in God's peace that we obtain the peace that passes understanding.

While we are musing, while we meditate, the fire kindles. The Holy Spirit operates in a way which is impossible in our busyness. Spiritual lives are developed in silence, where the deep things of our lives are shaped.—1973

AUGUST 31

John 6:9. *There is a boy here who has five barley loaves and two fish. But what are they among so many people?*

I spent a summer as a chaplain in a children's hospital. On my first day there I went to visit a little boy who had just had open heart surgery. He was not expected to live and was lying in the bed with tubes and monitors everywhere. He looked exactly like my own son. I looked at the boy and then I looked up at the father. He was rubbing his son's leg and a large tear was rolling down his face. I wanted to say something comforting or offer an eloquent prayer, but all I could do was cry. I just sobbed, and then the father began to sob, too. After a few minutes I managed a prayer and excused myself. I felt like a total failure. I was supposed to bring strength and all I had done was show my weakness.

It was a week before I had the nerve to inquire about the boy. To my delight I learned that he was recovering. I went to check on him and to apologize to the father.

He was there, smiling, and I said, "Hello." At once he began to thank me. My crying, he said, had made it OK for him to cry—something he never felt he could do. He said it was the greatest gift he had ever been given.

I had thought my offering was small and insufficient—like the loaves and fishes—but God knew better.—1996

SEPTEMBER

FORWARD
DAY
BY
DAY

AUGUST
SEPTEMBER
OCTOBER
2001

SEPTEMBER 1

Acts 12:21-23. *On an appointed day Herod put on his royal robes, took his seat on the platform, and delivered a public address to them. The people kept shouting, "The voice of a god, and not of a mortal!" And immediately, because he had not given the glory to God, an angel of the Lord struck him down, and he was eaten by worms and died.*

Maybe this petty little king suffered a heart attack at the very moment the people were shouting "The voice of a god!" The early Christians interpreted his fate as punishment from God because "he had not given the glory to God."

However we interpret it, we do well to remember that many people play at being God, as Herod did. It is so easy! And one need not be a Herod to do it. One need be only a plain, ordinary person who likes to tell other people how to live their lives. This is the essence of playing God: to demand that others accept our will for them. What makes things worse is that there's always someone who wants us to do the thinking and planning for them.

This may be everyone's number one temptation, to play God to others. Be on your guard against it, for it is easy and it feels good.—1962

SEPTEMBER 2

Acts 13:2-3. *While they were worshiping the Lord and fasting, the Holy Spirit said, "Set apart for me Barnabas and Saul for the work to which I have called them." Then after fasting and praying, they laid their hands on them and sent them off.*

Writer Lord Dunsany once said that the marks of the divine in a person are benevolence, extravagance, and song. They are the marks of the divine in the church, too. The primacy of benevolence and charity seem obvious. And the Christian church has always been a singing church—at the Last Supper, they departed after singing a hymn. But what of extravagance?

One way that extravagance is expressed is in foreign mission. Service in the overseas mission field is always a bit fantastic, beyond strict common sense, what the charts recommend, and what we say about how sensibly we shall settle the proportion between what goes abroad and what stays at home. The Holy Spirit said, "Set apart for me Barnabas and Saul," when there was every logical reason for them to remain at home. Mission in faraway places and among people we do not know will always seem extravagant, and for that reason it is divine, the mark of a true church.—1942

SEPTEMBER 3

John 9:37. *Jesus said [to the man who had been born blind], "You have seen [the Son of Man], and the one speaking with you is he."*

We cannot know the historical Jesus, and it was not the intention of the gospel writers to present him to us. Their message was the Good News of a God who is our contemporary, the living Lord of our lives. Through the message of these gospel writers written long ago, our Lord speaks to us in the here and now.

Furthermore, this living Lord uses other means, in addition to scripture, to reach us with the Word for our time. We cannot prescribe how or where God will speak to us. We cannot restrict God's movement or message. We can only be attentive to events and persons around us and faithful in our worship and study. If we are attentive, we, like so many before us, may find that this living Lord is much closer than we have ever imagined. The gospel writers saw Jesus and spoke with him. And, through their writings and other means, we too have seen him and have heard his voice speaking with us.—1983

SEPTEMBER 4

John 10:3-4. *He calls his own sheep by name and leads them out…and the sheep follow him because they know his voice.*

A little girl from Connecticut whom I know kept making a mistake when reciting the Lord's Prayer each night. Her version was: "Our Father, who art in New Haven, how did you know my name?"

The child's mother was troubled about the mistake and asked her pastor what she should do about it. The pastor replied: "I wouldn't correct her just now, for, after all, she has hold of two wonderful truths about God: God is everywhere, even in New Haven, and God knows her name."

There is good reason why we like to be called by name. In an impersonal world, to be called by name reminds us that we are individuals, each a sacred and unique person. In the relationships that mean most to us, we always call each other by name.

When Jesus wanted to draw a picture of God's love, he spoke of the way a Syrian shepherd treats his sheep: he calls each by name, and the sheep follow because they recognize the voice of the one who knows them and cares for them.—1965

SEPTEMBER 5

Luke 14:33. *So therefore, none of you can become my disciple if you do not give up all your possessions.*

I hear those words, but as someone living in a consumer society, I find them hard to bear. Then three images come to mind:

First, the statue of Saint Francis in my yard. It's amazing that so many admire this man whose stark insistence on poverty is so foreign to us. Maybe it's the bird on his shoulder. Or maybe we sense, deep down, that we're on the wrong track.

Second, I sat yesterday with a family in grief. They noted in irony that the deceased had bought a new car the week before and had been very proud of it—but how little it matters now.

Third, after reading to my sons, I hugged them and tucked them in. My older boy clung tightly and said he wanted to stay in my arms forever. I looked around the room. When my son comes down for breakfast tomorrow, I won't hesitate to close the door to this room. Its things provide a nice backdrop for living, but they aren't life. My son and I would be sorry to part with our things, but they are not what matters. Knowing that, we have, in a way, already parted with them, thanks to the grace of God.—1986

SEPTEMBER 6

John 1:39. *[Jesus] said to them, "Come and see. They came and saw where he was staying, and they remained with him that day.*

Christ's followers asked, "Where are you staying?" They weren't asking for an address—they wanted Jesus' presence. After all, John the Baptist had called him "Lamb of God," which meant to them that this man could bring forgiveness. Actually, they wanted far more than they could verbalize, and in replying "Come and see," Jesus meant far more than they could comprehend.

"Come and see" on Jesus' lips was an open-ended invitation for the day, for life, for eternity. Following Christ meant incredible change, as well as spiritual intimacy with Christ, identification with his name, suffering as his disciples, life in his risen power, and, ultimately, entry into God's welcoming presence!

Christ invites us, whatever our situation. Some of us simply hope for an uneventful day, or we may be longing for patience and strength to get through tomorrow.

Others are making life-changing choices that require wisdom. Some face a difficult diagnosis, unemployment, or homelessness. Prisoners lean into grace for living one enclosed day after another. We are all invited—bored, joyful, grieving, contented, anxious, depressed, healthy, impatient, or weary. Christ says, "Come and see." And he will give far more than we can verbalize. He offers far more than we can comprehend.—2013

SEPTEMBER 7

Psalm 48:8. *We have waited in silence on your loving-kindness, O God, in the midst of your temple.*

The story is told of one of the Desert Fathers (fourth-century hermits who pursued the life of holiness in the Egyptian desert) who was visited by the bishop of Alexandria. The bishop was searching for something edifying to take back to the city. The old man's disciple, anxious that the bishop be satisfied, was dismayed when no word whatsoever passed from his master's lips. After the bishop had left in disgust, the disciple asked his spiritual father why he had treated his visitor so. "If he is not edified by my silence, he will not be edified by my words," the old monk replied.

One of the hardest things to do is to wait, especially in silence. Yet if we cannot wait, if we are unwilling to remain faithful in silence, the word we hear will more likely be our own, springing from our anxious spirits, and having little to do with the quieter, deeper, and usually more radical word that is of the Lord.

Had the bishop been willing to wait and endure the silence, he would have heard a word not simply of edification, but of life.—1982

SEPTEMBER 8

Acts 13:47. *For the Lord has commanded us, saying, "I have set you to be a light for the Gentiles, so that you may bring salvation to the ends of the earth."*

We too must accept with joy the responsibility to speak the truth and to move beyond our comfortable places. We are to show our faith in God by our actions. This goes beyond our presence in church on Sundays. We must consider prayerfully ways to lift other people up. While ministering among them, we are to keep our own agendas fluid and flexible. Often we will be asked to give up certain ideas or plans for the greater good—ideas and plans that may be dear to us and that we may see as central. We may experience setbacks. But God calls us always to be open to what lies ahead, however it may surprise us.—1982

SEPTEMBER 9

Acts 15:10. *Now therefore why are you putting God to the test by placing on the neck of the disciples a yoke that neither our ancestors nor we have been able to bear?*

Peter raises this question at the First Council of Jerusalem. The same question could be asked in every church council and convention. We spend our time and energy debating budgets and programs, rules and regulations, who is in charge and who should determine what to do and believe. When we deal not with hundreds of disciples but with millions of church members, careful planning and recognized procedures become essential—we often get so preoccupied with secondary things that they begin to seem primary to us. How we must try God's patience! Anything in church life which stands between us and those with whom we should be sharing the gospel of Jesus Christ is a yoke upon our necks. As Peter also reminds us, "We shall be saved through the grace of Jesus Christ."

At that first council, the apostles put aside traditional regulations to reach out to people formerly excluded from the fellowship of the faithful—to the Gentiles. Do we have enough confidence in the grace of our Lord to reach beyond our national, cultural, and social boundaries to those outside our circles?—1965

SEPTEMBER 10

John 11:35. *Jesus began to weep.*

When Jesus heard of the death of his friend Lazarus, he did not speak of the world to come or tell a parable about the kingdom. He cried.

A colleague died of AIDS acquired from a patient. The patient was a child with hemophilia who had received multiple transfusions. Unknown to any of us, that transfused blood harbored the virus. The child began bleeding profusely one night and went into cardiac arrest. My colleague and friend was the first one on the scene. He resuscitated the child and was covered with the child's blood. It was his death sentence.

I was asked by my friend's family to speak at his funeral. I spoke of this verse: Jesus began to weep. Lazarus will rise from the dead, but Jesus weeps. Loss and pain are etched upon Jesus' heart and in his tears. Jesus knows our losses because he has experienced them. He will defeat death by walking through it, not around it, and not before he has tasted all its bitterness and anguish. He weeps for Lazarus, as I wept for my friend, and you wept for your mother, your father, your child. He has known our sorrow fully, intimately, painfully. He will deliver us from it, but he knows well from what he delivers us.—1999

SEPTEMBER 11

Philippians 1:27. *Live your life in a manner worthy of the gospel of Christ.*

It is hard to live in a manner worthy of the gospel of Christ. Just as you sit down to begin dinner, the phone rings. It is hard to resist wanting to jump right through the line and strangle the telemarketer. Or just as you head for the express checkout at the grocery, one of Christ's beloved pushes past you with 56 items. And a checkbook. With no checks. You obediently await your turn to board the plane and discover some other child of God sitting in your seat and there is no empty seat for you to move to. A flight attendant appears, another of God's beloved, and berates you for not being seated and buckled in and announces to the world how you are holding up departure.

It is the small, everyday events of life that most test our manner of living worthy of the gospel. Major emergencies, disasters, traumas, catastrophes—these can draw out the best in everyone. This is a good thing, of course, because those are times when we all need to work together for God's people and make it through. But wouldn't it be nice if people just treated everyone the way they would like to be treated?—2001

SEPTEMBER 12

Luke 15:2. *This fellow welcomes sinners and eats with them.*

Luke sets the stage for controversy between Jesus and the Pharisees and teachers of the law. Tax collectors and other "bad characters"—the down and out, the sinners beyond the edges of polite society—draw near to him. To eat with such folk was a cardinal sin in the minds of the respectable Pharisees. Jesus therefore goes "head to head" with them, using three parables: the Lost Sheep, the Lost Coin, and the Lost Son. These parables drive home a chief lesson of the gospel.

The first parable concerns a man of some means, the second a woman threatened with the loss of a significant part of her savings.

Jesus uses these parables in protest against "hard-liners" who say in their hearts, "God—and I—forgive you, but only on condition that you repent, and then only after proof of your repentance."

Over these parables write in large letters: "God's love for the outcast." God be praised that "this fellow welcomes sinners and eats with them." Who would these sinners be today? Who are today's outcasts? Or are the biggest sinners those who are not outcasts? With whom today would Jesus dine? Who are the lost sheep?—1983

SEPTEMBER 13

Acts 15:39. *The disagreement became so sharp that they parted company.*

It is almost with relief that we read about such things in the New Testament: even saints like Paul and Barnabas fell out with each other. All was not perfect peace and harmony between them. Barnabas wanted to take Mark along on their missionary journey; Paul did not. So sharp were their differences that they could not continue to serve together. It reminds me of the verse attributed to Brigham Young: To live with the saints in heaven is bliss and glory. To live with the saints on earth is another story.

But notice that Paul and Barnabas both continued with their work for their one Master. Often when we Christians quarrel we take it out on God. Or because we don't click with someone in our parish or denomination we stop supporting the church or find a different church. We need to see this as Paul and Barnabas saw it: we are not here to agree completely with one another, but to sink our differences, whatever they are, in our common service under our one Master. We must never let our quarrel with our brother or sister become a quarrel with God.—1962

SEPTEMBER 14

Philippians 2:10. *At the name of Jesus every knee should bend.*

T. Ralph Morton, in his book *Jesus: Man for Today*, examines the title "Lord" as applied by the first disciples in the first Christian creed. Morton says it does not convey to us today what it did to those who first used it of Jesus. For them it was no mere title of respect; they meant Christ was master of their lives. The term conveyed ownership of the whole earth; they meant Christ was the creator and giver of all things. Says Morton: "They were making a quite stupendous claim for him. They were saying Jesus was in the same relation to the material world as God is. And when the Jews talked in this way they did not mean only that God had acted in the beginning to get the whole thing going. They meant far more that: there was a continuous purpose at work in the world, and this was supremely manifest in human history."

We need to recapture this hopeful attitude to the world and to life in the face of today's confusion. Christians do not seek an escape from reality that denies life's enormous challenges, but to assert the triumphant Lordship of God in Christ.—1975

SEPTEMBER 15

Psalm 72:16. *May there be abundance of grain on the earth, growing thick even on the hilltops.*

In much of America, the grain is ripening and will soon be ready for harvest. Combines will lumber through the fields like giants, cutting and threshing. But in countries like Mali and Ethiopia, the soil is exhausted, neglected, and leached of its power, so that harvests— when there are any—are pitiful, and the people who live there are desperate. Even when we try to share our bounty, wars and corrupt dictators sometimes thwart our efforts.

But try we must. A people insensitive to others will soon perish. God will not long protect a people who turn their backs on God's poor. The earth produces enough food for every human being to eat, yet at least one child will die of hunger as you read this page.

Perhaps we need to spend more hours on our knees, praying for the will and the wisdom to do something about world hunger and that we will find ways to overcome petty tyrants who frustrate distribution. Perhaps we need to offer God ourselves, our souls and bodies, as a reasonable, holy, and living sacrifice to relieve the poor.—1992

SEPTEMBER 16

Acts 16:25. *About midnight Paul and Silas were praying and singing hymns to God, and the prisoners were listening to them.*

It was midnight for Paul and Silas in more ways than one. They had been brutally flogged and thrown into prison merely for healing someone in the name of God—and God let this happen to them.

But Paul and Silas were not complaining at midnight; they were singing and praising God. This made for a strange and unusual midnight. The prisoners heard them—and they must have marveled. Whatever this new religion was that had gotten these two men into such trouble, it also gave them an astonishing joy and courage. No wonder the prisoners listened.

The world always listens when we Christians sing in our midnight hour. What wins people to Christ is not our sound doctrine or our beautiful worship or our high moral standards. It is not our friendliness or our parish programs. It is the courage and joy which sings out from our souls when midnight misery descends upon us.—1962

SEPTEMBER 17

Acts 17:6. *These people who have been turning the world upside down have come here also.*

Many sincere church people today seem to see Christianity as a social stabilizer rather than as an insurrectionist movement. They often say things like: "In a world of constant and terrifying changes, we need some things that stay unchanged, to which we can anchor our lives; and why can't we find that blessed security in our religion?"

There is a sense in which they are right. God stands fast and changeless, and our only refuge is in the divine changelessness. But this world is always changing; it must. And Christians are to be revolutionaries making certain the changes conform to God's will. This is why the great Christians are always bent upon "turning the world upside down." And no sooner is a change made than someone finds a way to use the new order for ungodly ends. The world always needs turning upside down. We dare not accept things as they are. God commands us to go forth in his power to attack entrenched greed, cruelty, and godlessness. This means change. And Christians know how to turn the world upside down in such a way that God can set it right side up.—1962

SEPTEMBER 18

John 12:46. *I have come as light into the world, so that everyone who believes in me should not remain in the darkness.*

Early in the morning, I rose to see Venus, the morning star, in the east. She shone with a reflected glory, in advance of a greater light soon to come.

Later that morning, I visited a family in grief. A mother and father had lost a son in the war. He was their youngest. His unit had been ambushed; he had been killed. He was gone, struck down in the prime of his life.

The young soldier's father rose, too, on that Saturday morning. He wandered outside, as was his custom, and noticed the morning star in particular. While he prayed in his awkward and pained way, he was suddenly struck by something unexpected. Looking up at Venus, he heard the voice of his son: "I am here; I am here."

When the deep sky is dark, lights shine for our comfort and strength. They are signs in the sky which reflect a greater glory. This greater glory shines even when our lives are at their lowest. If we look for them, we can steel ourselves to deal with whatever comes our way.

Give thanks today for a light that shines in your darkness.—2006

SEPTEMBER 19

Luke 16:10. *Whoever is faithful in a very little is faithful also in much.*

Every time I am chained to a "little thing," I remember the day I set up chairs for a meeting to plan action against segregated housing. My wise rector noticed me chafing at the task. Gently, he reminded me that setting up chairs would help make the meeting possible and that, in my ministry as a priest, I would spend a lot of time doing such "little things." I knew what he meant: if I couldn't be trusted to care about little tasks, who would entrust me with larger tasks?

Let us keep little things in perspective, but let us also honor them. A Sunday worship bulletin, for example, is hardly cosmic, but it requires our best effort. Besides, what's little to me may not be so little to someone else. The way I greet a visitor on Sunday morning may rank 98th on my list that day, but it may make or break a church experience for the visitor. As a parent, I know my children will turn to me with "great" things only if they have learned through "little" things that I can be trusted.

God has much for us to do and to be, but first we must be faithful setting up chairs.—1986

SEPTEMBER 20

Luke 3:4. *The voice of one crying out in the wilderness: "Prepare the way of the Lord."*

Notice the slight difference in Luke's quotation from the original in Isaiah. It has to do with what takes place "in the wilderness." Isaiah had written (40:3): "In the wilderness prepare the way of the LORD"— the wilderness was where the divine highway was to be built. But Luke modifies it so that the wilderness is where the messenger cries out to prepare the way of the Lord.

There is truth in both versions of the saying. It is not just within the warm and friendly environment of our little circle of friends that we are to build the Lord's highway, nor is it only there that we are to speak in the Lord's name. Our calling—both to do and to speak—is in the wilderness, in the hard places, amidst the tensions and traumas of daily living.

Where is your wilderness? In a children's hospital where a little boy is dying of AIDS right before his parents' eyes? On the streets of the city where you live? In a small town that has been going downhill for years? In your own living room? Name your wilderness. That is where you are called to do and to speak in the Lord's name.—1994

SEPTEMBER 21

Matthew 9:13. *I have come to call not the righteous but sinners.*

Saint Matthew was a tax collector. In those days, that job called for a man who was a cross between a traitor and a profiteer. Matthew handled the idolatrous coins of the Roman Empire, as the agent of an unwelcome conqueror. He collected duties on merchants' goods for an employer who had bought tax privileges at public auction. This system made petty cheats out of everyone working in it. Everyone in this business was dishonest; no one was worthy to be a disciple of Jesus, a man who "had nothing."

And yet this same careful soul guarded the treasures of Jesus' sayings with an inspired economy and wrote them down. The same careful hand that once had taken the outrageous fees of the customs house now combed the Old Testament for references to validate the claims of the early church.

Jesus' power to see greatness in small men made small men great. Can a Christian ever say of anyone that he is hopeless?—1944

SEPTEMBER 22

Psalm 81:10. *I am the LORD your God, who brought you out of the land of Egypt and said, "Open your mouth wide, and I will fill it."*

Today I struggled on my daily walk on the beach. The sand was soggy, with water just below the surface. I had to watch my feet to prevent a misstep. On another day, I had turned and walked backwards to avoid the wind in my face and then taken a spill because I wasn't watching. This need for constantly watching where I walked made me think of how we approach life: do we look down at our feet to be sure we are walking safely? Or do we look backward remembering the past and then fall because we are too concerned with things done and left undone?

The future is always before us—bright, shining like the unspoiled beach—ours to make what we can of it. I'm not advocating forgetting everything about the past. God reminded the Israelites to remember God's faithfulness in the past so that they would be assured that God would be there in the present and future. But rather than be handicapped by regret, we are to remember all experiences that might help us live in the future.

There is risk ahead; there may be pain as well as good times waiting, but God is always with us to give us what we need to face the future and to fill us with what we most need.—1995

SEPTEMBER 23

Luke 4:18. *The Spirit of the Lord is upon me, because he has anointed me to bring good news to the poor.*

Snow fell on me as I waited for a cab. A rumpled homeless man in a stocking cap and fingerless gloves asked me for money.

I like to know that anyone I give money to is worthy (which usually means working or actively looking for work) and I don't want him spending the money on alcohol or drugs. So I donate through a church or community organization. Pastors usually encourage that kind of giving.

I gave the man twenty dollars because I'd just been to the ATM and had nothing smaller. He stared at me for a moment and stammered, "Ma'am? You meant to give me a dollar, didn't you?" When I said no, he put his head back and began to yell, "Thaaaank you, Jesus!" over and over. He went to a nearby coffee shop and came out with a huge cookie and a cup of coffee, still singing out, "Thaaaank you, Jesus!"

What if a beggar misuses my money? That isn't my business. Giving to a beggar is between me and God; what he does with the money is between the beggar and God.—2004

❧❧❧❧

SEPTEMBER 24

Luke 4:32. *They were astounded at his teaching, because he spoke with authority.*

This passage upsets many popular ideas about religion. Anyone who devoutly awaits the coming of God had better be prepared for trouble. You may discover that with God's coming you will drop everything, leaving your work, your family, and your possessions.

Then, in this passage, we find Jesus teaching with more power than the official teachers. There is nothing more disturbing to a professional than to be outdone by an amateur. And then, with a power not to be denied, Jesus proves his authority over the minds of people by commanding the unclean spirits.

In all such events, no one would offer the slightest objection if God were doing it. But here was a man (as they thought), untrained in divinity (as they thought), speaking and acting as if he had a right to heavenly authority. "Have you come to destroy us?" asked the man in the synagogue. Perhaps Jesus had. Perhaps he had come to destroy many things that had usurped a place not their own.

"Have you come to destroy us?" It was a natural question. It might well be our question, too.—1962

SEPTEMBER 25

Acts 20:16. *He was eager to be in Jerusalem, if possible, on the day of Pentecost.*

Despite the pressures of his missionary work, Paul was in a hurry to reach Jerusalem before Pentecost. Paul was deeply involved in his work with the young churches, yet it was important to him that he join the disciples at Jerusalem, even though he knew he would be in great danger there. Travel in those days was dangerous under any circumstances, yet Paul chose to travel.

Paul knew the strength of his ministry depended on his coming together with the disciples. It was in coming together for worship and the common meal (eucharist) that the disciples gathered strength and courage to preach the gospel of Jesus Christ to a hostile world.

How often do we hear, "Oh, I don't go to church often, but you don't need to go to church to be a Christian." The truth is, "being a Christian" is not something private. Our Christianity is expressed when we gather as a people to worship. It is in our coming together to rehearse the gospel of Jesus Christ that we strengthen our common faith. We are not merely individual Christians, but a Christian people. It is as a people gathered in worship that we find the sustaining strength that makes our faith a reality.—1968

SEPTEMBER 26

Luke 16:19. *There was a rich man who was dressed in purple.*

At a time when there was a striking division between rich and poor, the rich man's indifference to the poor man at his gate was not unusual. In fact, we all are surrounded by suffering in one form or another, and even if we do not live with the extravagance of the rich man in the parable, we do find ourselves, perhaps in self-protection, turning indifferently away from the pain around us. It is difficult for us to read this story without a spasm of guilt.

What was the rich man's sin? He did, of course, let a man lying outside his house starve for want of the bread which the rich man's guests used to wipe their fingers before flinging it onto the floor. He did not see this poor scarecrow of a figure, racked with pain and disease, persecuted by the dogs and doubtless by flies and heat. But more than that, he failed to see that the poor man was a man exactly like himself, that in a sense he was himself. What people sated with this world's goods choose is the hell of isolation, of being cut off from their fellow humans.—1976

SEPTEMBER 27

Luke 5:5. *Master, we have worked all night long but have caught nothing.*

Peter's words touch our own sense of emptiness when, after a great expending of energy in our work, family life, or ministry in the church, it seems little is gathered from our efforts. At that moment a simple act of obedience in response to the Word of God can transform the situation. Jesus did not tell the disciples to do something new or different—he simply said, "Go on. Try again. Don't give up." Any doubt or cynicism which Peter might have felt was dispelled when he obeyed. He was overwhelmed not just by a huge catch of fish, but by the presence of Jesus.

Instead of a change of vocation, lifestyle, church, or ministry, God may be inviting us to go on faithfully with our "ordinary" work, allowing that to become the place of epiphany. The French Jesuit Jean Pierre de Caussade once spoke of everyday duties as shadows beneath which the divine reality lay concealed. He encouraged his readers to recognize "the sacrament of the present moment"—that is, its capacity for making Christ visible. We only see the light of God as we take the shadows seriously by entering them. Live faithfully day to day and leave the results to God.—1989

SEPTEMBER 28

Luke 5:23. *Which is easier, to say, "Your sins are forgiven you," or to say, "Stand up and walk"?*

Jesus tells the paralytic that his sins are forgiven. The Pharisees are furious, charging blasphemy, because forgiving sins is God's business. So Jesus commands the paralytic to take up his bed and walk. The healing miracle does not prove that Jesus is authorized to act on God's behalf in forgiving sins, but it does present a challenge to the Pharisees. Can such healings be allowed if Jesus is an arrogant blasphemer who insults God?

We have been forgiven, too, in our baptism and many times since. But God's mercy may not be clear either to us or through us. Have we changed our behavior because we belong to Christ and have been forgiven in Christ? A life changed by Christ's action gives witness to those not yet believing. If we do our part in opening the way to God's will in our lives, we will be changed. Our changed lives may not bring anyone to believe in Jesus' forgiving power, but we do not know that. Someone's conversion may depend upon our starting to walk.—1990

SEPTEMBER 29

John 1:48. *Nathanael asked him, "Where did you get to know me?"*

Nathanael had been brought to Jesus by Philip, who first had prepared him to meet the man he thought must be the Messiah. Although not convinced, Nathanael was greeted by our Lord with the comment, "Here is truly an Israelite in whom there is no deceit!" Completely disarmed, Nathanael responded with the question, "Where did you get to know me?" It was easy from then on for Nathanael to follow Jesus. People like to feel that others think well of them.

But Jesus did not want an easy victory. Commitment required more than that. So following that brief exchange, Jesus told Nathanael that he would see much more before he was really converted.

Many people join a church because of the friendly interest shown in them by a church member. Christian conviction, however, is not easily gained. It comes after we really yield to the living Lord and experience his sustaining grace in the trials we bear. God always knows us; what is more important, do we really know God, through his Son, Jesus Christ?—1964

SEPTEMBER 30

Luke 6:2. *But some of the Pharisees said, "Why are you doing what is not lawful on the sabbath?"*

When I was young, my closest buddy attended a church that kept Sabbath from sundown Friday to sundown Saturday. Being separated on Saturday was a trial for us. His family's Saturday hours of prayer, reflection, and rest weighed heavily on his restless soul, and he spent much of the day watching the clock and imagining his friends running free in the neighborhood. My buddy's church had a lot of rules taken from the Old Testament, and as he grew up he broke most of them.

The early Christians not only celebrated Sunday as the day of the resurrection, but kept the Jewish Sabbath as well. Gradually, however, Christians let the Sabbath go, though many kept Sunday as a day of rest as well as worship. Until the second half of the twentieth century, it was illegal in many places for businesses to open on Sunday.

In Jesus' time the Sabbath law was both onerous and full of loopholes for the informed. But the idea was good, and as I look into the exhausted faces of the twenty-first century, I realize how much we need a Sabbath, and how little chance there is for most people to have one.—2003

OCTOBER

FORWARD
DAY
BY
DAY

AUGUST / SEPTEMBER / OCTOBER 2004

OCTOBER 1

Hosea 10:12. *It is time to seek the Lord.*

"Only believe!" says the preacher, but his words require qualification. We are called to more than mental assent to God's purposes. It is a mistake to think that God can bring us forgiveness, refine our nature, use us in the ongoing cause of the kingdom, if all we do is believe and passively wait. God calls us to active cooperation. The exhortation to the Israelites in today's verse means they were expected to play a part in their own redemption.

The work of grace in us is ultimately of God. Yet that work cannot be accomplished unless we also make some effort to achieve it. Christians of earlier generations described prayer and meditation as devotional exercise—something requiring energy and effort. How easily may our prayer life be impoverished if we fail to make conscious endeavor to preserve and deepen it!

Author Olive Wyon wrote: "If we have allowed certain elements in our lives to get out of proportion, if we are using our intellectual abilities too little or too much, if we are having too much sleep or too little, if we are underfed or overfed, if we are sitting up too late at night, or allowing some recreation or interest to become too absorbing—all these apparently irrelevant things will affect our prayer life."—1975

OCTOBER 2

Luke 6:31. *Do to others as you would have them do to you.*

Psychologists tell us that we don't really understand the wishes of our own hearts. In our desire to justify and rationalize our behavior, we "sweep under the rug" or bury in our subconscious minds desires both good and bad that are too disturbing to be faced.

Maybe this is why we have turned the Golden Rule into a simple, narrow standard that is easier to live with than the uncompromising command to love our neighbor. It is easy to say, "I wish only that my neighbor would leave me alone, and therefore I will do the same to him." Or "All I ask of my neighbor is what I give to her—decent courtesy and fair dealing in matters of business."

But deep inside we want a whole lot more than that. We show it in our quick response to anyone who seems to care about us personally. A thousand polite relationships cannot take the place of one real friend. What we want is love, and if we are to follow Jesus Christ, this is what we are required to give.—1964

OCTOBER 3

Luke 17:6. *The Lord replied, "If you had faith the size of a mustard seed, you could say to this mulberry tree, 'Be uprooted and planted in the sea,' and it would obey you."*

Was Jesus using exaggerated imagery to make a point about examining our faith? As Luke tells the story, Jesus was teaching about unlimited forgiveness. Perhaps because they found that a demanding word, the apostles asked Jesus, "Increase our faith."

Instead of giving them a formula for faith development, Jesus urged them to examine the faith they had. If their faith was real, its size wouldn't matter.

How can one evaluate one's faith? Tree throwing doesn't sound too promising. But boldness in living does.

As you face the stresses of living, do you see in yourself the audacity that would command a tree to be uprooted? Or do you see fear, a tentative drawing back from risk? Faith gives us courage to live boldly.—1986

OCTOBER 4

Luke 6:41. *Why do you see the speck in your neighbor's eye, but do not notice the log in your own eye?*

An earlier verse in Luke, "Do not judge, and you will not be judged," is sometimes misunderstood to mean that we can set no standards of behavior by which we govern our common life, and ought not protest against sin when it occurs. But to say that the fullest understanding of human action belongs to God is not the same as saying that we bear no responsibility for measuring, as best we can, our actions and those of others against Christ's law of love. It just means that our human judgment will be flawed. Only God's judgment is perfect.

Christians who ponder the morality of another must do so from a position of humility, an honest admission of personal vulnerability. God's judgment is absolute; ours is not. Human judgment has been shown to be mistaken, and the norms of one age are not those of another.

I cannot avoid ethical choice and moral evaluation, but I can avoid making absolutes of the contingencies that make up the parade of human life. They are not the eternal truth of God, only the arrangements by which we manage our walk through life on the way to that eternal truth. One day we will know it for what it is, and our minds and the mind of God will be one.—1994

OCTOBER 5

Psalm 120:5. *How hateful it is that I must lodge in Meshech and dwell among the tents of Kedar!*

Meshech is in modern day Turkey and Kedar refers to Arabia. This year we had an exchange student from Turkey living with us. We did not do this by plan. I always thought having an exchange student would be nice, but too much responsibility to add into our already hectic lives. However, Murat needed to change homes in the middle of the year and he had become a friend of one of our sons through soccer. This quiet, stoic student changed our view of the world.

Turkey is no longer a foreign country to us. There is a person named Murat whom we love now living there. As American troops are now being sent to the Middle East, I not only fear for my sons' being involved in a conflict, but I fear for Murat and his country's border with Iraq. If only we could think in terms of persons and families in other countries instead of troops and arms. We also realized through Murat what a difference one person can make in our world view.—1992

OCTOBER 6

Luke 7:24. *When John's messengers had gone, Jesus began to speak to the crowds about John, "What did you go out into the wilderness to look at? A reed shaken by the wind?"*

He stood at the door of the church office, a nondescript little man in shabby clothes. Since we were on a main street that was also a cross-country highway, there were a lot like him. "Could you spare a little change for a meal? Our car has broken down. Can you put us up for the night?" Sad to say, there are more such persons all the time.

Only he was different. He was poor, yes. On the road, a wanderer, yes. But he had stopped to ask a different question. "How is it with you, pastor?" At first I thought it was a come-on, more elaborate than most. But he had meant it. He crossed the country two or three times a year, stopping as the spirit moved him to ask people about their faith. Over the years, I probably saw him on eight or ten occasions. We had a lot to share.

He became a John the Baptist figure in my life, enough out of the ordinary to ask arresting questions. Eccentric. Not your usual preacher. Full of the Holy Spirit. Not what you'd expect. One of God's surprises.—1994

OCTOBER 7

Psalm 131:3. *But I still my soul and make it quiet, like a child upon its mother's breast; my soul is quieted within me.*

My spiritual director gave me this psalm to meditate on five years ago while she was trying to lead me through an Ignatian retreat. I am still working on it.

The psalm has become a great source of comfort to the inner child of my soul when she becomes scared and frightened. I read the psalm and feel a calm, nurturing, quiet, feminine part of God holding me very close. I am nurtured by a loving Mother beyond me, around me, and in me. My inner child can be calmed and quieted by a loving God.

Too often in a frenzy, as we occupy ourselves with things "too great," as we let our minds push our bodies out of balance, this child within cries out and we attempt to quiet her with food, alcohol, work-dependent relationships, or power. I am learning that only God knows best how to nurture this inner child. All of these other sources are "junk food."

There is a power greater than me constantly and lovingly caring for and carrying me—and you.—1992

OCTOBER 8

Psalm 142:1-2. *I cry to the LORD with my voice; to the LORD I make loud supplication. I pour out my complaint before him and tell him all my trouble.*

When my grandson Thad was two, we often looked at a little picture book. He especially liked a picture of children sliding down a slide in a playground. He wanted to play too, and tried stepping on the picture, saying "Get in there! Get in there!"

When I told his aunt Robin about this, she said that she used to try to get into the mirror like Alice in Through the Looking-Glass, and What Alice Found There. "But I always got in my own way," she said.

So often, "all my trouble" comes from my getting in my own way. So often, I try to make something happen, rather than letting God take care of it in God's own time. Other times I take the line of least resistance and fail to take the action that I need to take.

I so often get in my own way. And I feel like the writer of Psalm 142: "I look to my right hand and find no one who knows me; I have no place to flee to, and no one cares for me."

I can get out of my own way. I can tell God all my troubles and leave them in God's hands. If I do this, God will bring me out of my looking-glass prison.—1993

OCTOBER 9

Psalm 104:27. *And there is that Leviathan, which you have made for the sport of it.*

Asteroids, storms, centipedes, nettles, flounders, black holes, persimmons, people. Why does God make these things? Some say God creates because it is the nature of God to create. But that's like saying the sky is blue because it is the nature of the sky to be blue. Others say God creates in order to have someone to love. But that would seem to suggest that God is incomplete or unfulfilled without us to relate to.

I don't know why God creates. But I like the idea of this psalmist, who looks at one of nature's more implausible creatures, the whale (leviathan is Hebrew for whale), and suggests that God made it simply for the fun of it.

I like to envision God sitting wherever God sits and dreaming up things that will amuse him: "I think I'll make a funny little wingless bird and plop it down in Antarctica. Then tomorrow, I'll make the Amazon. The day after that, icebergs. Then I'll put together the Crab Nebula, and then grapevines. And then I'll make ocean waves, snowflakes, sunbeams, blueberries, and quarks. Then, for the sport of it, I'll make a huge sea creature that blows air out the top of its head. All this I shall do, just for fun! Then I'll make human beings and let them wonder why I did it all."—2001

OCTOBER 10

Luke 17:15. *Then one of them, when he saw that he was healed, turned back, praising God in a loud voice.*

Recently our son's pet hamster died. We knew it had to happen sometime, but there was no way to prepare our son. There never really is a way to prepare for how we will feel in the face of a loss. So we prayed that God would help us to feel better, that we would be comforted. And then my son went one step further. He told me that he had said "thank you" to God for his pet.

That was when the real healing began. His gratitude for a gift— beyond his anger or sorrow at his loss—was beginning to make him whole.

Sometimes we have to give thanks before we are healed in order to become whole. We give you thanks, almighty God, for all the benefits you have given us, you who live and reign forever.—1991

OCTOBER 11

Acts 26:1-2. *Agrippa said to Paul, "You have permission to speak for yourself." Then Paul stretched out his hand and began to defend himself: "I consider myself fortunate that it is before you, King Agrippa, I am to make my defense today against all the accusations of the Jews."*

It is an elderly lady who has spent two years in bed, often in great pain, who says, "Every night I thank God for my blessings. People have been so good to me." It is Scrooge's clerk and his son Tiny Tim who say, "God bless us, every one."

Thanksgiving does not depend on the outward circumstances, but on how we take these circumstances. A tragedy can embitter or ennoble. That is up to us.

Most often we are only thankful if we get things our way, and in this we have left out the greater half of thanksgiving. We have forgotten to be thankful for opportunities.

Paul stands alone before Agrippa, a prisoner caught in the iron grip of Rome. He faces imprisonment and death. He does not complain. He thanks God for the opportunity to speak to Agrippa about the risen Christ.

Let us not bewail these days of change and danger, but thank God for these stirring times of new adventure and new opportunities to spread the power of Christ's truth.—1942

OCTOBER 12

Luke 8:50. *When Jesus heard this, he replied, "Do not fear. Only believe, and she will be saved."*

Sometimes faith is all we have. It certainly was for me, the night before my big operation. As the evening wore on and the end of visiting hours drew nearer, my friends and family began to drift towards the elevators. When I was alone, I decided to take my mind off the life-altering experience of the next day by watching a hockey game on TV. Wouldn't you know it? My team lost. After that I was tired (or perhaps drained) enough to want to go to sleep.

Before I drifted off I prayed, and in doing so was granted the peace and comfort I had sought throughout that day. The day had started with my signing an indemnity form absolving the hospital of any responsibility for my possible death, paralysis, or other injury or disability as a result of the operation. It then carried on through a series of medical tests and preparations, and ended with the visits that left me stripped bare emotionally. From a quiet prayer, however, I found myself spiritually girded with the armor that I needed to face the unknown and the darkness of what would be eleven hours of unconsciousness and surgery.

Just believe.—2003

OCTOBER 13

Luke 9:17. *All ate and were filled. What was left over was gathered up, twelve baskets of broken pieces.*

In this grassy, lonely place the crowds have assembled to hear Jesus speak. They are without food. With five loaves and two fish Jesus feeds them all.

It may sound silly to say that one finds some miracles easier to understand than others; once we have allowed that the miraculous can occur, then it is hardly for us to pick and choose the ones we prefer.

But I find this miracle harder to make sense of than ones that concern physical and mental healing. Mind and body are so intimately connected that it is not difficult to believe that contact with a whole person, such as Jesus, might have a profoundly creative effect upon the sick. But this miracle suggests that God is as present in the atoms that make up bread or a fish as God is part of the matter and the spirit of a person who believes in him.

Every bit of created matter is within God's disposal. And as one might guess from the way the world has been ordered, God is no ascetic. God does not send the crowds fasting to their homes, but gives generously, even extravagantly. There is food left over. Joy in food, and the goodness of the body which lives upon it, seem inextricably a part of the best Christian tradition. That is why giving thanks is so important.—1976

OCTOBER 14

Luke 9:23. *If any want to become my followers, let them deny themselves and take up their cross daily and follow me.*

What does it mean to deny one's self?

Picture yourself entering a gathering of people. Family, friends, or strangers—it doesn't matter. You can enter filled with self or empty of self.

If you're filled with self, you think every eye is on you as you enter. You seek like-minded people. You turn conversations to your own interests. You try to impress. You're "on." You're selling. You avoid disclosing any "negative" emotions like fear or anger. Is it working? You can tell by how you feel. Sound familiar?

If you're empty of self, you see the needs of other people. You're available to whoever comes near. You draw out other people. They feel larger in your presence. You affirm. You share. Is it working? You look for clues in the other person's eyes.

The self-emptying scenario sounds better, doesn't it? Why, then, don't we live this way? It's risky. It's often painful. But more than that, it requires intentionality. That's what strikes me about Jesus' own self-emptying. He planned it out in advance. He worked at it. We, too, need to be intentional about our lives, our faith and our self-denial.—1989

OCTOBER 15

Luke 10:8-9. *Whenever you enter a town and its people welcome you, eat what is set before you; cure the sick who are there, and say to them, "The kingdom of God has come near to you."*

The kingdom of Nepal, in which Mount Everest and many other high Himalayan peaks are located, is officially a Hindu country. It is against the law to preach conversion to any other religion. However, it is not illegal to heal the sick, to treat lepers, to help the poor, to teach, or to run a model farm. Since the 1950s, Christian missionaries have gone to Nepal to do these things. In that time, because of the way these dedicated men and women have lived and worked, many people have learned about Jesus, and a number have become Christians.

The most effective form of evangelism is one's way of life. Other people are more impressed by what we do than by what we preach. Pray that you might live your life in such a way that others may be attracted to Christ.—1983

OCTOBER 16

Luke 9:46-47. *An argument arose among them as to which one of them was the greatest. But Jesus, aware of their inner thoughts, took a little child and put it by his side.*

Edward Chinn, author of *The Wonder of Words*, tells the story of a little boy whose talent as an artist attracted the attention of a psychologist. "When he visited the boy's home, he was both astonished and puzzled; astonished by the excellence of the boy's work, but puzzled by the fact that the paintings covered only half their canvases. He tried several indirect questions to find out why the boy painted this way. Finally, he asked him straight out, 'Why do you always leave the top half of your paintings blank?' The boy replied, 'Because I can't reach that high!'"

The child knew his limitations but he did not miss any of the possibilities. This is a good parable of our vocation as disciples. Some may be "greater" in talent than others, but we all are called to be as creative as we can be, knowing that the "top half" will be completed by the One who has called us to be co-workers.

Do you think Jesus had something like this in mind when he set forth a child as a model for his disciples? What a relief not to have to worry about the blank spaces!—1987

OCTOBER 17

Genesis 32:24. *Jacob was left alone; and a man wrestled with him until daybreak.*

The life of God cannot be grafted on to the stalk of our humanity without surgery.

The rite of Holy Baptism makes this clear, although the point is often missed in our tendency to sentimentalize this ancient rite. The death unto sin which this sacrament implies is a drastic process indeed. The hardiness of human nature is not all to the good unless brought under subjection to the higher task of living unto God. And that subjection involves the pruning shears and the surgeon's knife. Our will is not strong enough without God's will. Our love is not pure enough unless caught up in God's love. Our best is only an imperfect flower unless it be expressed through God.

And like Jacob in today's lesson, we can't wrestle with the angel without limping a bit afterward. Our encounter with God always leaves a scar—a reminder that whatever of Christ's life is expressed through us comes at a price for him, and for us too.—1958

❧❧❧❧

OCTOBER 18

2 Timothy 4:11. *Only Luke is with me.*

We are grateful for Luke the physician who set forth in his gospel the love and healing power of our Lord Jesus Christ. Who could do it so sympathetically as one who himself ministered to the sick?

According to scholars, we are in all probability indebted to Luke not only for his unique gospel so rich in the story of our Lord's birth, but also for the first Christian church history, the Acts of the Apostles.

How faithful, how earnest and untiring was this life to which we pay tribute today! Only the unfailing companion of Saint Paul could have known in such detail the story of the great missionary expansion of the early church.

This is a good day for us to resolve to be ambassadors of the love and healing power of Christ.—1944

OCTOBER 19

Matthew 7:14. *For the gate is narrow and the road is hard that leads to life.*

The gate that leads to the chapel is very narrow indeed. Only one person can squeeze through it at a time.

And once inside the only residential Anglican seminary in southern Africa, the road can be hard for many who have answered God's call. Many students are poor. Some have traveled far to get here and seldom see home and family. A student from Haiti has not been back home for three years.

While here, one student became head of his family when his mother died. He traveled home to bury her and to send a sister to live with relatives in another country. One student received word that her mother was terminally ill; another's daughter had brain surgery. When her sister-in-law died, another student and her relatives took the woman's three children into their own families.

Yet through it all, we saw God's presence as the students ministered to one another. Collections were taken, prayers were offered, tears were shed, and all manner of assistance was provided as the entire community responded in love. They were all walking that hard road together.—2014

OCTOBER 20

Luke 10:23-24. *Blessed are the eyes that see what you see! For I tell you that many prophets and kings desired to see what you see, but did not see it, and to hear what you hear, but did not hear it.*

Not long ago, I heard a particularly good performance of Mussorgsky's popular *Pictures at an Exhibition*. The music was composed to make listeners "see" the pictures Mussorgsky saw as he wandered through the art exhibition. I couldn't conjure up in my mind the pictures described in the program, but the sounds were eloquent. I did hear something very special, and I "saw" other things meaningful to me.

What we see and hear inwardly gives meaning and direction to our lives.

As someone said, "The gospel is not a philosophy, not even the affirmation of a universal truth; it is the proclamation of a concrete and unique event, which sets the whole meaning of human life in a new light through the Incarnation."

In Jesus' life and teachings we can see what the true nature of God is, and we can hear and understand what is truly important to know. Only look and listen; insights for life and action will follow.

L.P. Jacks was right: "The radiance of the Christian religion is not lost; it is simply not yet found." Keep on searching until it is.—1988

OCTOBER 21

Matthew 13:55. *Is not this the carpenter's son?*

Jesus must have seemed ordinary. People didn't look at him or listen to him and say, "This man is God." He didn't radiate light or float over the ground. He bled when he scratched his toe and laughed when he was tickled. People who had known him from childhood had a hard time realizing he was special. Was he not the carpenter's son?

This may seem unimportant, but when people forget it they are led into some foolish ideas and behavior. Some suppose that Jesus never laughed and therefore consider laughter to be "unspiritual." Others trying to follow him move with studied grace and speak in "holy" tones. Still others reject the God-filled life because they could never bring themselves to act "like that." Some cannot imagine a divinity in ordinary human form at all.

Many pious people forget that they can ask God to be with them in their silly, embarrassing, or awkward moments so that even those moments can be transformed by God's presence. That is important. God-filled moments may, like Jesus, look ordinary, but their inner reality is very different.—1988

OCTOBER 22

Luke 10:42. *Mary has chosen the better part, which will not be taken away from her.*

Jesus loved both Mary and Martha with the same outpouring of generosity he showed to all. And each of the two sisters responded to him with all she was and all she had to give. Busy, bustling Martha, scrubbing and polishing, slaving over a hot stove to make something special for the beloved guest. Mary, rather quiet, rather withdrawn, offering him her whole attention, listening and absorbing his words, watching his face.

Jesus accepted the offerings of both natures, and it wouldn't have occurred to him, probably, to praise one more than the other, for each expressed the reality of her own personal style.

It was Martha who forced the comparison. "Here I am doing all the work, and there she sits." And Jesus, gentle and good humored, but firm, made it clear that Mary had a part to play in the world— her work of contemplation—as legitimate and useful as Martha's. For her, even if not for Martha, it was the better part.

The peace and fruitfulness of your life is in being fully yourself.—1970

OCTOBER 23

Luke 10:33. *But a Samaritan while traveling came near him; and when he saw him, he was moved with pity.*

Who is my neighbor? The injured man in this story of the Good Samaritan is not identified. We know nothing of his race, color, creed, or background. Moreover, he was a stranger. Only one thing counted—he was in need and the Samaritan (a heretical Jew, by orthodox standards) responded. Anyone and everyone, known or unknown, who is in need is my neighbor.

Jesus pushed aside artificial criteria. How best can I satisfy others' just wants? This, he said, is the heart of the law and the prophets.

Many times he broke the Jewish law in order to answer a need. In the parable of the Pharisee and the tax collector (Luke 18:9-14), the Pharisee, for all his observance of the law, was condemned because he did not love, but despised, others.

Often it is hard to know exactly what love requires. Our diverse backgrounds and inherited prejudices warp our judgment and are subtle and powerful deterrents to action. Even tradition and custom can get in the way. But what wonders would take place if we demanded of our elected representatives that human need, rather than self-interest, be the only criterion in politics, in social welfare, and in international relations!

The world waits. And we, what are we waiting for?—1967

OCTOBER 24

Luke 18:13. *But the tax collector, standing far off, would not even look up to heaven, but was beating his breast and saying, "God, be merciful to me, a sinner!"*

Unlike the Pharisee's self-congratulatory gaze at his own reflection, the tax gatherer opened himself to God. It was a painful moment. Opening ourselves to God often is a painful process.

Whereas the Pharisee sounded like a proud employee reporting to his boss to receive his pay, the tax collector threw himself onto God's mercy. He knew his failings. He knew his need for forgiveness. He seems also to have known God as merciful. Unlike the Pharisee who related to God in terms of ancient rules, the tax collector seems to have related to God as a personal God living in the present.

I am struck also by the difference between the Pharisee and his list on the one hand, and the tax collector and his beseeching on the other. In approaching God with lists in hand, whether they are lists of successes or less prideful lists of failings, we may miss the heart of prayer. The point of prayer isn't to inform God, but to open ourselves to God.—1986

OCTOBER 25

Psalm 44:1. *We have heard with our ears, O God, our forefathers have told us, the deeds you did in their days, in the days of old.*

Will and Ariel Durant, in their book The Lessons of History, remind us of the importance of an open study of the past. "To those of us who study history not merely as a warning reminder of man's follies and crimes, but also as an encouraging remembrance of generative souls, the past ceases to be a depressing chamber of horrors; it becomes a celestial city, a spacious country of the mind, wherein a thousand saints, statesmen, inventors, scientists, poets, artists, musicians, lovers, and philosophers still live and speak, teach and carve and sing."

God has worked through such people, and their example, instead of being a "depressing chamber of horrors," becomes for us light to lighten our own road. We need this perspective of the past. This is especially true in a sophisticated age such as our own, when relevance to the demands of the present so often seems to dominate our thinking. It is good for us to recall how God has worked in that spacious country where saints and poets and lovers have lived, where they have taught and carved and sung. This can help us to see God at work in our own day.—1972

OCTOBER 26

Psalm 48:1. *Great is the* Lord, *and highly to be praised; in the city of our God is his holy hill.*

In every land there are holy places, places of pilgrimage, places which people have visited to encounter God. It is part of our religious instinct to set places aside for God. There are dangers in this—people can assume that God shuns the other parts, outside the shrines. But there are elements of truth too. We need to be reminded. We aren't always aware of holy things. We forget God, or take God for granted.

Or, like fools, we say, "How shall God perceive it; is there knowledge in the Most High?" No, we need to be reminded. So we have shrines, churches, crucifixes. They bring certain facts to mind.

To the Jew who first sang this psalm, the holy hill was where God dwelt. For me it may be the spire of some village church which for centuries has pointed its finger to the heavens. I shall never forget standing outside the Kremlin in Moscow, with the tower near the gate surmounted by the hammer and sickle that could be lit up at night. Beside it and above it, in inexorable courage, towered the spires of the churches with their crosses on top, dominating the city and pointing a reminder to all who saw with eyes to see that this God is our God for ever and ever.—1967

OCTOBER 27

Luke 11:38. *The Pharisee was amazed to see that he did not first wash before dinner.*

We know of a priest who spent a weekend visiting a parish, talking with the people and taking the Sunday services. Afterward a parishioner was asked what his impression was of the minister. "He must have fallen asleep after the sermon," he replied, "because he didn't even bow in front of the altar as he went back to his seat."

Of that whole weekend during which this man had much contact with the priest, the only thing he commented on was a most insignificant point of ceremonial custom. There was no particular need to face the altar, God being in just about any direction. We are always in such danger of letting some little thing obscure what a person really is. And very often the more sincerely religious we are, the more insidious the habit of nit-picking.

Jesus denounced the Pharisees in some pretty strong language for doing this very thing. He would do the same to us if we concentrate only on the petty details that keep us from the important things. Like people.—1971

OCTOBER 28

John 15:17. *I am giving you these commands so that you may love one another.*

Of all the words that we fling around, surely "love" is the most battered. We praise it. We identify it with the very essence of God—and then throw it away, usually with carefully explained reasons. Anger. Being misunderstood. Even being confused. All drive us from love. I'm not talking about accepting abuse. I'm talking about that love that heals the broken, comforts the afflicted, and also challenges the self-righteous and the complacent.

As Jesus' followers—his friends, as he says—we are asked to love one another, holding together in a world that is not always friendly, that, in fact, crucified him. But instead we stop talking to our families, gossip, hoard our gifts—or deny them. "Oh," you say, "I'm friendly with everyone." Well, there are dangers. For instance, how is love shown in Christ's community, the church? I know someone who left a parish because a cross wasn't carried in the gospel procession. People who use incense complain about those who don't. Some are drawn to penitence, others to celebration. Gospel music, plainsong, or traditional hymns? Catholic or protestant? Women's roles? Men's? Clergy? Lay? It can often seem like it is my interpretation vs. theirs.

What does this have to do with love?—1992

OCTOBER 29

Psalm 51:11. *Create in me a clean heart, O God, and renew a right spirit within me.*

A saint is not a person who has achieved perfect goodness, but one who has come to desire it with his whole heart. Is the righteousness of God your chief desire? If so, you will not be one of those who object to the General Confession in the [1928] Book of Common Prayer. You will find it helpful to join with others in saying "there is no health in us."

Humanity's great tragedy is willful isolation from God. Whatever separates us from our God, making our hearts cold and our wills unresponsive, is sin. In the confession, we admit our need for God. We ask God to show us our sins of commission and omission, that we may turn away from them and come into blessed union with God. Why should you shrink from referring to yourself as a miserable sinner when it is sin, and only sin, that makes you miserable? God alone, through Christ, has the power to purify us, provided we desire to be cleansed. Try saying over and over during each day, "Create in me a clean heart, O God, and renew a right spirit within me."—1938

OCTOBER 30

Psalm 139:1. *You know my sitting down and my rising up; you discern my thoughts from afar.*

God not only is near us, God knows us. God knows us better than any human person could possibly know us, even our own family. This is the God "from whom no secrets are hid." When we pray, we can be sure we are not telling God anything God does not already know. We do not have to explain or excuse or dissimulate before God. We can be ourselves as we can be before no one else.

The psalmist knew this, although he believed God was "afar." God had not yet come to earth in the person of Jesus Christ. The psalmist thought of God primarily as creator and helper, all-powerful and all-knowing. Christ taught us to know God also as a loving father who, if we will let him, will be with us and in us and a part of us always to help us become like him.

And so, because God knows us and is near us, we can talk to God and pray to God with the assurance that he really does hear us and knows us and is with us.

All of this seems very simple and hardly worth saying. But when we find ourselves neglecting our prayers, we might well ask ourselves if we really and truly believe that God knows us and hears us at all times.—1957

OCTOBER 31

Luke 19:10. *For the Son of Man came to seek out and to save the lost.*

Few of us in the early twenty-first century hear much from the pulpit about being "lost," about sin or sinning or our personal status as sinners. The mainline churches gave that up a generation or more ago, and even the most zealous evangelical groups are more prone to preach the "prosperity gospel" today than any word about human sinfulness and how that applies to us.

Less than a century ago, sinfulness and the dreadful eternity awaiting those who wallowed in it was a common theme for preachers. Now, the emphasis is on God's love and acceptance of us. That is a lot healthier, but we shouldn't forget why Jesus came to live and die as one of us.

We are all sinners; none of us deserves God's love. And yet God does love us in spite of our sins. There is a problem when we take forgiveness for granted, when we don't try to overcome our sinful proclivities. Jesus accepted sinners, but he did expect them to repent. To err is human, to forgive divine; to strive to do all that God asks of us is our duty and our joy.—2005

NOVEMBER

FORWARD
DAY BY DAY

NOVEMBER / DECEMBER 2006 / JANUARY 2007

NOVEMBER 1

Luke 6:29. *If anyone strikes you on the cheek, offer the other also.*

Being wronged does not give license to retaliate with another wrong. Our Lord speaks strongly when he says that we shall not resist the evildoer and that whatever the wrong deed done against us, we must suffer the deed again and again.

By refusing to retaliate, we teach the wrongdoer that we are not vindictive. If we were vindictive, we would be poisoned with the same evil spirit that governs the wrongdoer.

Christ tells us that revenge is not as satisfying and sweet as one would imagine. We can often bring about a mutual understanding by refraining from vengeance. This does not mark us as cowards. Rather, we become victorious because we do not allow ourselves to be lowered to the level of the offender. We also know that the offender may change his attitude and behavior with an example such as this before him. One thing is certain: We can do ourselves more harm than anyone else can do to us if we let anger and hatred overcome us.
—1960

NOVEMBER 2

Luke 13:2-3. *[Jesus] asked them, "Do you think that because these Galileans suffered in this way they were worse sinners than all other Galileans? No, I tell you; but unless you repent, you will all perish as they did."*

Why do calamities happen to some people and not to others? Were the poor Galileans who were slaughtered at the altar or the men on whom the tower of Siloam fell particularly wicked?

Investigate any earthquake or tornado, and you will see that the relatively innocent suffer with the relatively guilty. Jesus speaks of repentance, but he does not threaten the unrepentant with the fate of those Galileans. He simply reiterates the Old Testament warning: in some way every person who defies God will perish. Not because God wishes it so, but because there is a moral order in the universe.

This is only one side of our Lord's teaching, but it is the necessary background of the Good News. Without judgment, forgiveness would be meaningless. What the Bible calls the "wrath of God" is also the love of God; it is the word that brings correction to God's children. Otherwise it would not be love at all but sentimentality that makes no distinction between right and wrong.—1963

NOVEMBER 3

Luke 13:12. *When Jesus saw her, he called her over and said, "Woman, you are set free from your ailment."*

A leader of the synagogue pointed to the woman with the evil spirit. To him, she was nothing but an object lesson. He rebuked Jesus, pointing out that there are proper times for healing and that the sabbath day of rest is not one of them. Jesus, however, ignored the rules because here was someone in need. Neither did he philosophize about how people took precedence over principle or sermonize about how specific needs close at hand are more important than abstract causes. He simply healed the woman.

One of the ways we keep people at arm's length is by putting them in groups. Then they become abstractions—old people, young people, racial groups, national groups, political groups, conservatives, liberals. Whenever we box people into groups ("You know how they are!"), we protect ourselves against personal encounters that may seem threatening to us but which are essential to Christian love. It is impossible to love an abstraction. Not Jesus! He said to the woman, "You are freed from your ailment."—2000

NOVEMBER 4

Luke 13:24. *Strive to enter through the narrow door; for many, I tell you, will try to enter and will not be able.*

Jesus knew and said that living faithfully would not be easy. We who are young or middle-aged are going to know this in ways our elders have never known. Christianity has been an accepted religion in the past. This will not be so in the years to come. Why?

First, we are entering a highly scientific age in which there will be great and rapid change. The church has usually been slow to change—in fact, it actively resists change. But now we must get on with it. Second, the church is beginning to engage the world in ways which past generations have neither known nor approved. At times we seem to be living in days much like our Lord's—the end of an age was approaching and a new era was being born. Out of the old religion of the Jews there came a small band, misunderstood, resented, and persecuted. But they lived a new and intimate life with God. The door to this life was narrow, but through it God brought forth a new thing for his people. It appears God may now be doing this again.—1967

NOVEMBER 5

Luke 14:13-14. *But when you give a banquet, invite the poor, the crippled, the lame, and the blind. And you will be blessed, because they cannot repay you, for you will be repaid at the resurrection of the righteous.*

My son came home with empty pockets after his first no-parents outing with friends. When I asked about the change from the convenience store, he said he had given it to the cashier. Mom, he said, she looked like she needed it more than me.

Nearly every day, I see people asking for money or food or work. When my children are with me, they always admonish me to give, even if we just helped another person a block earlier. I know it's not possible to give to every person on the street who asks. Many social workers say that this is not even the best way to help, that my money would be better spent in donations to charities that work for long-term solutions.

But I pray to be like my son, to listen to the still, small voice, and when the urge to give doesn't go away, to respond in generosity and with good spirit.

"Let not the needy be forgotten, O Lord. Nor the hope of the poor be taken away." Amen.—2016

NOVEMBER 6

Luke 14:11. *For all who exalt themselves will be humbled, and those who humble themselves will be exalted.*

Jesus was outspoken against doing a commendable deed for self-elevation. He rebuked those who entertained wealthy friends in order to be entertained by them or to receive their support. Giving with a selfish purpose is not Christian; it may not even be giving. This is important in a day when much emphasis is put on knowing the right people, having contacts, and playing up to those who have pull. Have you ever done something because it was the right thing, even when you knew it would deny you a desired preferment?

Pray that God will implant within you a desire to do what is right, not just what is expedient. Pray that he will help you love everyone and that you avoid "using" people.—1972

NOVEMBER 7

Psalm 98:5. *Shout with joy to the L*ORD*, all you lands; lift up your voice, rejoice, and sing.*

In the large city church where I worship, if you ask people what first attracted them to the parish they often say it was the music. Our people sing with energy. Hymns are songs of praise and prayer.

Sometimes, when it's hard to find the words to pray, singing or even speaking the words of a hymn does the trick. When small groups gather, people are often too shy to say an opening or closing prayer, but when you ask someone to open the hymnal and read a verse of a favorite hymn, it's another story. Words put to music enter our memories more readily and are remembered far longer than words alone.

At a funeral it is often a hymn that loosens us up and allows the healing tears to flow. In a nursing home, a familiar hymn can bring a smile to the face of an Alzheimer's patient. And during the church year, the hymns teach us about the seasons. The occasional worshiper who stares blankly ahead while others sing is missing something of great power. Sing to the Lord!—2006

NOVEMBER 8

Luke 14:12. *Do not invite your friends or your brothers or your relatives or rich neighbors, in case they may invite you in return, and you would be repaid.*

I invited a mendicant Buddhist monk into my home to live for several months. His saffron robes made quite an impact on our small English village. It was a very broadening experience. As he lived only by what others gave him, and as he could only eat what he was going to eat that day by noon, I had to rush back from work to cook a meal and place it in his bowl. Everything went into the bowl: salad, steak, and generally a Mars bar perched on top.

According to his tradition he could not thank me for what I gave him "because that would be the end of my reward." If he didn't thank me, my reward would be the greater because it came from a higher service. This is exactly what Jesus says in today's gospel reading. It was true. I did receive a greater blessing because I understood more clearly what Jesus meant. Jesus seems to be saying that we can limit what we get in life by going for the consolation prize rather than the fuller life that God has to offer. We are not to be like the hypocrites who fast in public and have their reward in full, namely, to be noticed. God's reward means doing all things in secret so that they collect heavenly interest.—2004

NOVEMBER 9

Psalm 78:20. *Can God set a table in the wilderness?...Is he able to give bread or to provide meat for his people?*

Here it is again! The old "what have you done for me lately" theme. In spite of the mighty works God has done to enable his people to escape from Egypt, in spite of his providing them water from the rock, they are ready to doubt God's ability to save them when they experience the first pangs of hunger. That we have a tendency to forget blessings and to nurse grievances is a palpable sign that we have a way to go before we are truly what God intends us to be. On our journey through life we need way stations where we can receive comfort and strength from him. When we are wandering in the desert, alone and aching, God's table in the wilderness is real: the altar, bread of life and wine of joy.—1996

NOVEMBER 10

Luke 15:2. *This fellow welcomes sinners and eats with them.*

Before we rush to condemn the Pharisees as disdainful snobs, let's remember that their attitude, as far as the law is concerned, is the correct one. The law-abider, the serious student of the scriptures, was obliged to separate himself from people, things, and experiences that would compromise his holiness. The Pharisees were understandably confused and upset by Jesus' insistence on engaging the sinner rather than shunning the sinner. Jesus no doubt would have argued that saving sinners was part of the tradition, too—but was it his reading of the scriptures, his religious tradition, that determined his actions? I doubt it. Jesus embraced the outcast simply because that is what perfect love does. When we scorn the down-and-out, it isn't respect for scripture and tradition that is working in our hearts—it's fear. The Pharisees were afraid—of losing their sense of closeness with God and the sense of rightness and order that came along with it. A religious life based on finely screened sacred texts usually leads to fear. It stifles. Jesus, on the other hand, lived freely and joyfully.
—1986

NOVEMBER 11

James 1:5. *If any of you is lacking in wisdom, ask God.*

Christians of the twentieth century, scattered abroad in many tribes and nations, to James, Christian of the first century: Greeting. Your letter reaches us across the centuries with meaning you perhaps could not have foreseen. No doubt it is always true that the moral life is strengthened by adversity and that a devout and unwavering faith in God brings the wisdom a person needs to live in adversity. We need that reminder as much as our ancestors did.

But some of us have less adversity to strengthen our souls than others. When you speak of the lowly and the rich, you remind us of the contrasts in our own time. Millions are starving while surplus food rots in storage. This is the scale on which moral problems are written in our time. Private vices and public crimes continue, but the real crime for us is global, and the rights and wrongs are multiplied by millions of individual decisions and complicated by politics, economics, and enough "isms" to tax the wisdom of all Christendom. The green grass fades, and the rich will wither away. But how shall God advise a wealthy nation that claims to be the hope of the world?—1960

NOVEMBER 12

James 1:17. *Every generous act of giving, with every perfect gift, is from above, coming down from the Father of lights.*

The meaning of this verse is obscure in some ways, but one thing is clear enough: Temptation cannot come from God; everything that comes from God is good. If we find this a pious platitude, perhaps we haven't examined it carefully. Some things that God either sends upon us or allows to happen to us do not seem to be good—they don't taste good, they are bitter pills. And our faith undergoes one of its most severe tests when we are asked to believe that the Father of lights, our loving Father in heaven, is allowing us in his mercy to suffer some bitter disappointment or sorrow or affliction. But James knew what it was to suffer for the Lord's sake, and he saw in that suffering a means of grace, a blessing from on high. In all our troubles we must be sustained by that faith. Whatever comes down from the Father of lights to us is good, and if we will trust him for the final issue, we shall one day see the goodness and rejoice in it.—1972

NOVEMBER 13

Revelation 2:29. *Let anyone who has an ear listen to what the Spirit is saying to the churches.*

Each of us is made in the Creator's image and has ears to listen. God is active in the world, and the Spirit speaks. We are invited to listen with our own ears and be moved by what the Spirit is saying to our communities.

When we listen to others who are also listening to the Spirit, we often learn to see something from a different perspective. We are enriched by listening to others who also listen to the Spirit.

None of us individually is big enough to receive and understand the whole of what the Spirit says.

Together, we can help each other hear more of God's message. God made us for each other and to answer the call to listen, as in all things, we need each other.

In some ways, we need those who are different from us the most, because they offer new perspectives to us. Getting to know people who are different from us through traveling to, living with, and doing mission work in new communities is one way to enlarge our perspectives.—2015

NOVEMBER 14

2 Thessalonians 3:10-11. *Anyone unwilling to work should not eat. For we hear that some of you are living in idleness, mere busybodies, not doing any work.*

The first Christians were real people, not figures made of stained glass. Sometimes we look back to those days as through a small and distorting telescope. We imagine that life in the early church was one long worship service, that those first Christians sat around for hours listening to sermons on justification by faith. But then we read a line in one of the epistles that brings us back to reality: there were lazy, idle busybodies in the church in those days, just as today. Church discipline was often lax and misunderstood. Someone was always confusing piety with laziness and trying to make idleness look like holy meditation. There is something worse than that, too: even sincere Christians are tempted to think of themselves as suffering for Christ, or even as martyrs, when it is merely that the sermon is too long or the pew uncomfortable. We know the person of whom Saint Paul was writing in this passage. He is still with us, perhaps in the pew next to us. Perhaps we are that person.—1960

NOVEMBER 15

James 2:17. *So faith by itself, if it has no works, is dead.*

Saint Paul taught that we are made right with God through faith, not through good works. If what we have here is a rejoinder from James to Paul, then we must say that James misunderstood Paul. Paul never thought of faith as mere intellectual adherence to orthodox doctrine, as James seems to suggest. For Paul, faith is total self-giving to God. If Paul is the object of James's castigation in this passage, we must enter a plea of "not guilty" for Paul. However, a large army of Christians down through the ages, and including the present, are guilty as charged in James's indictment: guilty of the great unconscious heresy of substituting creed for deed.

Playwright George Bernard Shaw said that a person's real creed is that body of beliefs on which he habitually acts. Let us examine our actual behavior, as seen in our thoughts, words, and deeds, to see what beliefs our behavior does in fact express. There may have to be some changes made if Christ is to be the basis of our behavior. We truly believe in Christ when his Lordship is manifest not only in our creedal profession but also in our habitual actions.—1972

NOVEMBER 16

Luke 17:10. *When you have done all that you were ordered to do, say, "We are worthless servants; we have done only what we ought to have done!"*

The analogy that comes to mind is parenthood. Some parents live through their children. Hungry for applause themselves, they push their children into applause-producing situations. But isn't the essence of parenthood found in the 2 a.m. feeding? No applause there, just a duty that goes with the role. When the baby grows up and becomes an applause-producer, some parents may consider the acclaim their reward. But I wonder if the real reward wasn't experienced years ago in that early morning feeding. The reward was the wholeness that comes from living the moment fully and authentically.

Life brings duties. Our roles bring duties. Some are pleasant; some aren't. We can't pick only the pleasant and ignore the rest. Bedtime story-reading may feel cozy, but 2 a.m. feedings are just as necessary for life. Living as a Christian isn't all 2 a.m. feedings, but it does have some of those no-applause moments. I think those no-applause moments give Christian living its flavor. When I give in order to get, my giving means little. But when I give selflessly, I live into my calling and thereby honor the one who called me.—1986

NOVEMBER 17

Luke 17:16. *He prostrated himself at Jesus' feet and thanked him.*

I remember the importance my mother put on writing thank-you letters and saying "Thank you" after a party. I recall thinking as a youngster that she made too much of it. I identified with the small boy who said after a party, "My mother told me to tell you I had a very nice time." Now that I'm grown up, I realize how important gratitude is. The name of our central service of worship—the eucharist—

means "thank you" in Greek. As a psychotherapist, I realize that the cornerstone of mental health is a thank-you attitude toward life, even in the midst of pain and less. Unhealthy is a whining "I deserve better than this; it's not fair" even in the midst of plenty. The ability to give thanks is a watershed of spiritual and mental health. To find a thank-you in your heart toward the Author of life is true worship.

Reflect on the area of your life that is causing you pain right now. Can you stay with the pain for a moment and sincerely say "Thank you" for something you have discovered within it? In doing so, you have just celebrated eucharist in your own heart. P.S. Thanks, Mom. —1995

❧❧❧

NOVEMBER 18

Luke 17:33. *Those who try to make their life secure will lose it, but those who lose their life will keep it.*

Jesus warns the disciples to prepare for a future encounter with Christ. The verse quoted above is most important: the more we try to get for ourselves, the more we are bound to lose. By unselfish service we attain Christian joy as a byproduct. If we actively seek peace of mind, spiritual serenity, and a good life, these things prove elusive. They are byproducts of an active life of Christian service that seeks nothing for itself.

Prayer suggestion: Pray for imagination and vision in finding new ways to serve God and those you meet daily. As ideas come during your prayers, write them down. Do not hurry through your devotions. Compile a list of acts of service you propose to do for others. Place it as a bookmark before chapter 23 of Luke's gospel, then check on it and evaluate it later.—1972

NOVEMBER 19

James 5:9. *Do not grumble against one another, so that you may not be judged.*

Some people fret and complain that the Christian pulpit intrudes itself into the social order and speaks evil against national leaders. But remember how Jesus followed the prophets in their eager concern for the dispossessed. It is futile to inculcate in the minds of our young people the ideals of Jesus and then send them into a world uncongenial to those ideals. Critics call upon the church to let business alone. But business and industry and politics do not let the people of God alone. Can the church stand by and see people cheated of the abundant life, pushed under the level of subsistence, in squalor, ill health, and occupational diseases? If it were a question of economics, the church might well leave the matter alone. But moral questions are involved. It will be a sorry day for the church if she ceases to be involved in human welfare.—1936

NOVEMBER 20

James 5:13-14. *Are any among you suffering? They should pray. Are any cheerful? They should sing songs of praise. Are any among you sick? They should call for the elders...*

Today's readings deepen our understanding of prayer. The stress is on living a life of prayer, not on the separate items of our intercessions. The value of all prayer is that it helps mold a life turned toward God and dependent on him.

In the gospel parable (Luke 18:9-14), Jesus contrasts two attitudes toward God. The Pharisee is pleased with himself and his works. Therefore God must be pleased with him. The publican knows he is a sinner. The first expects a reward; the other asks only for mercy.

A life of prayer excludes self-congratulation. James describes three situations. When suffering, we are to pray; when cheerful, we are to sing songs of praise; when sick or impotent, unable either to pray or to sing, we are to lean on others, depending on the prayers of those who also lead a prayerful life.

The prayer of faith is identical to a life of faith. Openness toward God and one another, dependence on others' prayers—these are aspects of a life of prayer. They are not separate items, but a single, indivisible state of spiritual health.—1978

❧❧❧

NOVEMBER 21

Colossians 1:20. *Through him God was pleased to reconcile to himself all things.*

Sometimes joy springs up from deep within us when we least expect it, catching us by surprise. We think of it as a gift, and so it is. But surely we are meant to develop this gift in ourselves. The source is always there, whether we are attending to it or not. God is always energizing the universe. Each moment holds out to us, in some form, the possibility of participating in Christ's work of building, of gathering to a greatness, of reconciling all things in himself, drawing all things to their own perfection, in God.

This discovery of joy has hardly begun to be explored. How much of our life we waste in tamer moments, feeling only a surface interest, a habitual and meaningless pleasure, nothing that goes deep. We must go deep. We must work at it, develop our own ways of seeing and attending, finding the joy that is there. This is a way of contemplation in the midst of the active life. If we take that path, it will open out before us into an increasing fullness of joy, a way of extreme delight.—1970

NOVEMBER 22

Luke 18:22. *Sell all that you own and distribute the money to the poor.*

"Shop until you drop," or retail therapy, is a popular way of responding to a case of the blues. This is a kind of "self Christmas," which means giving myself lots of presents in order to affirm that when the chips are down "I love me." This self-indulgence doesn't work and only produces an emptier bank account and an even emptier feeling inside. Jesus reverses the process, suggesting that we go on a giving spree—giving everything we have. It will not only cheer us up in the moment but also for eternity because it gives us entrance into the kingdom of God. In order for us to receive what God has to offer, our hearts and our lives must be empty. Sometimes we purposely empty our lives as Jesus counsels the rich man; sometimes our difficulties empty our lives for us. Either way, when the richness of God flows into an empty space, we feel fulfilled.—2004

NOVEMBER 23

Luke 18:38-39. *Then [the blind man] shouted, "Jesus, Son of David, have mercy on me!" Those who were in front sternly ordered him to be quiet.*

This blind man, perhaps to be identified with Bartimaeus in Mark 10, wanted to see, more than anything in the world. When Jesus the wonder-worker came along, he was ready. He set up such a clamor that his friends tried to hush him, but that only made him call more loudly, trying to attract Jesus' attention.

How often when we want something are we willing to make noises about it, roll up our sleeves and take action? Surely if all the people who claim to want world peace, an end to hunger, or justice for the oppressed were willing to shout to get attention and then act by approaching those whose help they need, more would be accomplished. "God helps those who help themselves" may be a cynical assessment of God's power and desire to act in our lives, but there's truth in those words. If we sit quietly and refuse to call on God or move toward him as the source of our help and strength, we will never be helped. The power is there. How long will it take us to decide to use it?—1988

NOVEMBER 24

Psalm 130:1. *Out of the depths have I called to you, O Lᴏʀᴅ; Lᴏʀᴅ, hear my voice.*

Easy good nature was one of the marks of the age out of which we are passing. We presumed to be easy-going with God. We thought that having improved ourselves so much, it was no great step to be in God's amiable company. We puffed ourselves up with the saying: "Every day, in every way, I am growing better and better."

Then the bubble burst. Four hundred delegates convened in Oxford in July 1937 for the World Conference on Church, Community, and State. The leader of the Conference wrote to the delegates, saying in effect: Do not dare come to Oxford in any mood of self-confidence. The present state of apostasy and frustration calls for whole-hearted repentance. Only out of a deep distrust and despair of self can the word be spoken which the world needs.

Do not think it morbid to be in the depths. Every sinner must begin there. And knowing oneself to be there, rather than skimming gaily in the shallows, is a healthy sign. The first step in repentance is for the sinner to know he has no dignity left. All that is left is a cry. But God never yet failed to hear and answer a cry out of the depths.—1939

NOVEMBER 25

Psalm 100:3. *Enter his gates with thanksgiving; go into his courts with praise; give thanks to him and call upon his Name.*

Thank you, Lord, for sharp cheddar cheese, a good night's sleep, that I have learned to take my opinions less seriously, for parishioners who have forgiven my foibles and helped me grow beyond them, winter wind and summer sunshine on my cheek, maps and atlases, the Body and Blood of Christ given for me; for Brahms symphonies, windows that can be thrown open at night, friends who love me enough to confront me with the truth I'd rather ignore, shoes that fit just right, strong black coffee, my three sons, mangoes right off the tree, front porches with swings, children who come to communion with hands outstretched; milkweed pods with a thousand silky seeds, oatmeal creme pies, the feeling in my chest after I have run and showered, work I love, my parents' faith in God and in me, the memory of being afraid or depressed or confused and that you stood with me then and will again; and thirty-four years with the right woman and all the times she has bailed me out, steered me right, given me another chance, and generally put up with me. For these and all your mercies, Lord, your holy Name be praised.—2002

NOVEMBER 26

Luke 19:37-38. *The whole multitude of the disciples began to praise God joyfully with a loud voice for all the deeds of power that they had seen, saying, "Blessed is the king who comes in the name of the Lord!"*

How does such a person as Jesus become powerful? Not by deliberate search and accumulation but by the kind of person he is. He is the person in whom others place confidence. People know that the inner resources of this person will endure. He does not need a bodyguard or a protective fence that a less secure person might have. This person is powerful even when riding a donkey at the head of a parade marching toward the capital, or riding in an open limousine in a city filled with hate, or standing unarmed and unflinching before a sheriff and his posse demanding justice for all citizens. The royalty resides in the person not in the position.

Shakespeare provides tragic pictures of men who are kings but who are not kingly, who have a crown but no power. Yet we see other men who are "every inch a king," even in their poverty, suffering, or death. The secret is inward power, that power which really influences, wins, and commands. Such power belongs to the person with an inner certainty that she or he is doing God's will.—1972

NOVEMBER 27

Philippians 2:4. *Let each of you look not to your own interests, but to the interests of others.*

Here is my favorite non-biblical parable: A man was taken on a tour of both heaven and hell. In hell he was shown a banquet hall filled with diners seated at a table laden with the choicest food. Each person's back and left arm were tied to the chair so that bending at the waist was impossible and the left arm could not move. The right arm was stiffened so that the elbow would not bend. The diners gazed at and smelled the food just inches from them, but they were starving.

In heaven the picture was the same—backs and left arms shackled, right arms stiffened—but the diners were feasting and rejoicing because each diner used his stiffened right arm to feed the person to his right. "Let each of you look not to your own interests, but to the interests of others."—1980

NOVEMBER 28

Matthew 24:44. *Therefore you also must be ready, for the Son of Man is coming at an unexpected hour.*

To be ready when Jesus comes again is a test, and the promise of his return can trouble us. We are made up of many rooms. We let some people in as far as the anteroom, others into the living room, and some into the dining room and kitchen. Old friends might even help with the dishes. A select few may enter our bedroom. But we also have that inner chamber where no one enters, which no one sees; our houses have no analogies for that. What we keep there is our own business—private thoughts, fantasies, plans, and behaviors that we're careful not to disclose. In the rest of the house we put out whatever we pretend to like, but here we gather our real treasures, the evidences of our real selves and beliefs. And into this room, one day, with fear and embarrassment and hope, we will invite our Lord. "It's not straightened up," we say, "and I've been meaning to have it done over; don't look at the dust—I've been so busy!" "Never mind," Jesus says, "I know. I am not surprised. I've been here many times before. Did you not notice me?"—1962

NOVEMBER 29

1 Corinthians 10:17. *Because there is one bread, we who are many are one body, for we all partake of the one bread.*

The young girl asks me a question, her eyes wide with expectation, awaiting my response. But I do not know the language she speaks. I am on the other side of the globe in completely foreign surroundings. I stand still, moored by her inquiry, an obstacle amidst the swirl of marketplace activity: the stench of butchered meat, the buzz of flies, the clank of coins, the insistent squawks of vendors hawking their wares. Aggressive patrons elbow, jostle, push past me in their urgency. I strain to understand her.

She touches the bottom of her neck, at that tender hollow below the base of her throat. There hangs a tiny, metal cross—a charm, a talisman, a tattoo of her baptism, glinting in the sub-Saharan sun. Then, she reaches out toward me, her fingertips landing on the tiny, gold cross at the base of my throat. My breath catches in comprehension. Across time and space, collapsing barriers of culture and language, we smile at each other in sisterhood.—2015

NOVEMBER 30

Matthew 4:19. *And he said to them, "Follow me."*

After you have repented, turned away from whatever consumes and fascinates and confines and controls you, and turned toward the Lord Jesus, then what?

"Follow me." Jesus' words are few, simple, and direct. It is not complicated. My mother-in-law, a woman of profound but clear and simple faith, said that no one was ever converted after the first seven minutes of any sermon; therefore no sermon should last more than seven minutes.

How often we complicate the call of Jesus with our intellectual constructions and behavioral rules! Jesus sums it up in just two words: "Follow me." There is little more to say after that. Repent, then follow Jesus.

Karl Barth, whom many say was the greatest Christian theologian of the twentieth century and whose published works fill several shelves in any good theological library, was interviewed as he departed the United States for his native Germany. Would he, could he sum up his theology in a few words? "Why, yes," he replied. "Jesus loves me, this I know, for the Bible tells me so."

Follow Jesus.—2002

DECEMBER

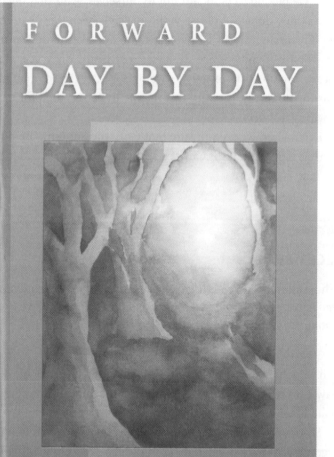

FORWARD

DAY BY DAY

FEBRUARY / MARCH / APRIL 2011

DECEMBER 1

Psalm 14:1. *The fool has said in his heart, "There is no God."*

There are two kinds of atheism. The first is an atheism of the head: an intellectual conviction that there is no God. The psalmist is concerned with the other kind, that of the heart. This is the atheism that wants no God.

Be honest. Isn't there a streak of this atheism in all of us? If God exists, we belong to God and not to ourselves. And that means that we can't just do as we please with our lives, because we are not our own. Fortunately, Jesus Christ steps into our lives to deliver us from this worst difficulty. Once we have truly heard his voice, we know that we can't just do exactly as we like. Whatever we may make of Jesus theologically, the very fact that he lived and died for us makes us belong to him.

Even when we are not sure that God, the Supreme Being exists, Christ is here. And Jesus Christ leads us to God, to life and to perfect freedom.—1963

DECEMBER 2

1 Thessalonians 3:7-8. *During all our distress and persecution we have been encouraged about you through your faith. For now we live, if you continue to stand firm in the Lord.*

Here we see beyond Paul's strong front, the strength and driving faith which inspired so many. Paul is admitting that he needs to draw energy and spiritual renewal from the faith of this community created by his energy and his faith.

So often we forget the endless exchanging of spirituality which is going on in a Christian community. We envy others' faith, certainty, awareness, and strength, when some of the time others may themselves be drawing their strength from us, from what we consider our own very ordinary and sometimes shaky faith. With all our limitations we are unwitting witnesses, sometimes to those we never dream would need us as resource. A marriage, struggling for a time, recovers and deepens, while wife and husband never know that in the process they strengthened others.

We never know how frequently, if we stand firm, others are given grace from our wrestling with our weakness and problems.—1982

DECEMBER 3

Psalm 16:1. *Protect me, O God, for I take refuge in you.*

Nighttime can be daunting. It's so dark. If we are worried, the problem is often worse at night. Often if something is bothering me, it's easier to cope in the daytime when it is light than in the dark nighttime. But I am armed now with prayers and scripture. As this psalm says, "I will bless the Lord who gives me counsel; my heart teaches me, night after night." In the beautiful service of Compline (*The Book of Common Prayer*, page 127) there are many comforting prayers and lines: "The Lord Almighty grant us a peaceful night and a perfect end," the service begins. And my favorite: "Keep watch, dear Lord, with those who work, or watch, or weep this night, and give your angels charge over those who sleep." And finally the antiphon, "Guide us waking, O Lord, and guard us sleeping; that awake we may watch with Christ, and asleep, we may rest in peace."—2006

DECEMBER 4

Romans 10:10. *For one believes with the heart and so is justified, and one confesses with the mouth and so is saved.*

As he got older, my father's hands became a trifle arthritic, and he loved it when we gave him hand massages. In fact, he extorted them. Parental favors were magnanimously granted in exchange for hand rubs, over which we would talk, sometimes about religion. My father was a priest who was magnificent at raising Christian children because he allowed and even encouraged us to voice doubt.

Most sources agree that belief is the major requirement for Christians. So when I first questioned my faith, it was frightening. My father taught me that in a skeptical world filled with thousands of religions and anti-religions, it becomes acceptable, even necessary, for strong Christians to question their faith sometimes. He gave me room to figure out what it means to believe. I can think of no better way to help a child grow into a mature Christian.

I would have rubbed his hands without borrowing the car. He would have loaned me the car without the hand rub. Probably.—2016

DECEMBER 5

Matthew 3:2. *Repent, for the kingdom of heaven has come near.*

The invitation to Holy Communion in Rite I of *The Book of Common Prayer* begins, "Ye who do truly and earnestly repent you of your sins, and are in love and charity with your neighbors, and intend to lead a new life..." For those who would be followers of Christ there is an urgency to change: from bad to good, from the "old man" to the "new man," from complacency to devotion. And yet, is not this urgency to change the very thing that our heart resists? How delightful are the courts of Status Quo. How satisfying the state of somnambulance. Or so many think.

Whether it be the individual Christian, the local congregation, the church at large, or the nation, there is no real communion with God without change. If we want things to remain as they are, we are telling God to be quiet. Repentance goes against the grain. Change is sharper than the pains of childbirth. An intention to lead a new life is the farthest thing from the mind.

But if you would see God, you must repent, you must change, you must intend something better than the life you are living. You can be just as you are if you insist, but isn't it hell?—1966

DECEMBER 6

Luke 21:28. *Now when these things begin to take place, stand up and raise your heads, because your redemption is drawing near.*

Folks in biblical times thought the end of the world might well be lurking in the next thunderstorm. Consequently, they weren't big on long-range planning.

In our time, we tend toward the other extreme. We've seen groups of misguided Christians march off into caves and coal mines to await the end of the world—an end which hasn't come yet, and which, given the easing of the nuclear threat, seems further away than we once imagined. But we would do well to raise our heads and see the plight of our less fortunate brothers and sisters, to determine how we might be God's instruments for peace and justice.

Let's not take comfort in the fact that the end of the world may not come for another ten million years. Instead, let's be a loving friend to that bothersome neighbor who will surely cross our path today! —1994

DECEMBER 7

1 Thessalonians 5:17. *Pray without ceasing.*

In Willa Cather's novel *Death Comes for the Archbishop*, two things stand out about the archbishop's prayer life. The first is that he always read his prayers before he got out of his sleeping bag. He had learned that his prayers were never prayed unless they came first, before the routine and business of the day. That is one good reason for having set times and places for private devotions. Without discipline, the practice breaks down and our separation from God grows greater.

The second thing about the archbishop's prayer life is that he experienced great periods when he knew not the presence of God. But he continued to pray. During one such period he discovered the childlike faith of a very simple old woman. It was her devotion that restored for him the refreshment of fellowship with God.

When our reservoirs run low and when God seems distant, God can speak to us through another person's faith and thus restore our relationship. —1953

DECEMBER 8

Psalm 38:22. *Make haste to help me, O Lord of my salvation.*

Our job is to witness to what the Lord has done in our lives. The Lord's job is to take our witness, grand or simple, and use it to get to the heart of the one hearing us. Many times a witnessing believer is surprised at how the Lord uses some simple incident or phrase to change a hearer's life.

Witnessing is the most natural thing. You fall into conversation with someone who brings up a problem or concern. As you converse you remember how God helped you with a problem of your own. You share that incident. Even if you fumble with words and are certain you have made a grievous mistake, God will use your witness to encourage that person to come to him.

As in this psalm, the prayer may be as simple as "Hurry up and help me, O Lord!" It is not the perfection of witness but the action of the Lord that makes the difference. Ask God to provide you with opportunities for witness today. You'll be surprised.—1978

DECEMBER 9

Psalm 37:26. *I have been young and now I am old.*

I like being older, and I surprise myself by saying this. One is supposed to shove aging into the closet and lock the door.

I like this stage of my life, not so much because I can sleep late if I wish or because I can play with my grandchildren and then send them home to their parents. It's because of what my friends and I talk about. Twenty years ago we would have discussed the fate of the university football team and whose child got into which college.

Today we will talk about death, prayer, the mystery of God. Such subjects would have seemed morbid or too personal then. Now they seem immediate and inviting and worthy of sharing. In the sharing we honor one another's humanity and cherish the time we have together. And, in the process, God's precious gift of friendship assumes a sweet intensity we might not otherwise have known.—2006

DECEMBER 10

Luke 22:19. *Then he took a loaf of bread, and when he had given thanks, he broke it and gave it to them, saying, "This is my body, which is given for you. Do this in remembrance of me."*

I remember a Christmas Day in a small country church. There were only about fifteen of us in the congregation, and at the offertory the priest invited everyone to stand around the altar for the celebration of the eucharist. As we gathered, I noticed the bread was not lying on a paten, the usual plate used in communion. Instead, it had been placed in a small manger from a Nativity set.

There we stood, gathered around the altar on Christmas morn with the bread from heaven lying in a manger. "I am the bread of life. Whoever comes to me will never be hungry" (John 6:35). These words of Jesus recall his birthright. The King of Heaven came to dwell with us and spent his first night in this world lying in a feeding trough. The world took little note that night. But as the deeper hungers of life could not be filled or satisfied with the things of this world, some did discover the nourishment he offered.

On Christmas it is well to come to the feeding trough—the manger—to feed our hungry souls.—2000

DECEMBER 11

Luke 22:33. *And [Peter] said to him, "Lord, I am ready to go with you to prison and to death!"*

When Peter promised to stay with Jesus even unto death, Jesus knew he meant well. But Peter was human. Like us, Peter fell short of his promise.

The promises we make during Advent—to amend our lives, to be loving and forgiving toward others—often fall short of our best intentions. With God's help, spiritual growth and renewal may occur.

More likely we will be overwhelmed by the demands the world makes on our pre-Christmas piety. It may be that we will begin to dread Advent and the whole seasonal rush and confusion leading up to Christmas. Or, just maybe, we will learn not to seek so much to be different for a season, but seek to be different for a lifetime.

If Peter can be pardoned by our Lord, any of us can be as well. Whatever we promise, whatever we do, whatever we hope must and will be finished in Jesus. Alone we are lost; with him it is enough.—2000

DECEMBER 12

Matthew 11:2. *John heard in prison what the Messiah was doing.*

In the depths of despair, the imprisoned John the Baptist sent several of his followers to ask one of the most important questions ever posed, "Are you the one who is to come, or are we to wait for another?" Jesus told them to tell John "the blind receive their sight, the lame walk, the lepers are cleansed, the deaf hear, the dead are raised, and the poor have good news brought to them." Yet the things Jesus did and the words he said are not nearly so important as the person who did and said them—the person whose love was so strong, whose personality was so dynamic, whose mission to all was so imperative as to drive him ultimately to the cross.

Jesus lives and works the miracles today which he worked twenty centuries ago. Remember that Christ is here now. How are you going to respond to him?—1952

DECEMBER 13

Luke 22:42. *Father, if you are willing, remove this cup from me; yet not my will but yours be done.*

Christmas is eleven days away. Everywhere preparations are underway. The choirs, pageant players, the altar and flower guilds are all working nonstop. In the church office there is a fever pitch as Christmas letters and extra bulletins are designed and produced. In the nave, the manger scene is beginning to fill with sheep and cows and an occasional shepherd, all there to await "the event." So why, as we prepare to remember and celebrate the birth that changed the world, are we reading of Jesus as he kneels in fearful prayer in the garden of Gethsemane?

As we prepare for Christmas, why are we reminded Jesus will go to the cross, suffer, and die? Without the rest of the story, Christmas could become an over-sentimentalized feast about Jesus' humble birth. Christmas is about the power of divine love—love which comes among us to be born and will go to any length to save us. As we prepare, let us never forget the complete salvation gospel.—2000

DECEMBER 14

Luke 22:57, 62. *"I do not know him"...And he went out and wept bitterly.*

Peter, as Jesus predicted, denied him three times. Peter is like many of us: upfront, outspoken, impatient, intolerant, sometimes unreliable, and probably difficult to live and work with. He fought and failed yet was able to pick himself up and start over again. Peter's core faith in the person and the promise of Jesus grew and deepened despite the setbacks. He persevered for Jesus' sake, as well as his own. Why can't we do the same?

Faith is not a predictable phenomenon. It has its ups and downs. Every day I have to redefine my faith in terms of its depth, health, and constancy. Every day I need to look anew at Jesus and myself and our relationship. Faith is a volatile, vibrant, ever-changing, deepening sense that Jesus is God incarnate and that his birth and life and death and resurrection testify to who God is. But like love between two human beings, spiritual relationships change. Good relationships mature and deepen as people grow up. Relationships define reality rather than the other way around. "For a child has been born for us" (Isaiah 9:6). We need to take Isaiah's words literally and personally. Then we will know Jesus and know our Prince of Peace has really come!—1998

DECEMBER 15

Psalm 119:62. *At midnight I will rise to give you thanks, because of your righteous judgments.*

Midnight has come and gone. I am wide awake. Sleep gave way to worry hours ago and now seems unlikely in spite of my weariness. My mind is filled with worries, from sermons to shopping. I am not ready. Too many plans, too many preparations, too many details remain. I sit and stew, pace and pout. Prayer? Not practical. What I need is time—more time. I flip through the stack of unread magazines. I pick up a book and put it down.

Prayer? In the morning at my "appointed time." I look in the refrigerator. I look out the window. I look everywhere but inside, because inside is such a mess, and I need order. I look at the Christmas tree. It looks dry. That fits. Me and the tree—all decked out and drying out. As I kneel to fill the bowl beneath the tree, the moonlight shining through the window falls on a silver ornament—a manger with parents and child. It glows, and I remember what is real. Thank you, Lord. Sleep or no sleep, because you sent us your Son, this is a good night.—2003

DECEMBER 16

Psalm 33:11. *But the Lord's will stands fast for ever, and the designs of his heart from age to age.*

"The Lord's will" can seem a heavy phrase, suggesting some plan for our lives that we cannot know, conceived in the inscrutable mind of God. More than once I have prayed for guidance, just a hint of direction, when facing an important decision. But God's will for me is usually no clearer after the prayer than before. Occasionally I've been sure of God's will (or thought I was). Then I faced a different task—trying to pump myself up with enough courage, strength, faith, will, or whatever, to go out and do it.

I don't know which makes me feel worse—not knowing God's will for me, or knowing it and failing to do it. Either way, God's will feels like a burden I can't shake off: either way, I lose.

The second part of this verse suggests a different understanding of God's will. Perhaps it is a matter of the heart, of what God longs for, rather than what God wants us to do. Perhaps God is less concerned about where we work, whom we marry, what we do and say, and our outward circumstances than about the orientation of our hearts. Perhaps his deepest desire is that we simply enjoy the pleasure of his company and invite him to enjoy the pleasure of ours.—2001

DECEMBER 17

Matthew 11:3. *Are you the one who is to come?*

From prison, with execution near, John sends a messenger to Jesus to ask this question. Near the end of his life, he wants to know that his ministry has meant something; that he will not die without seeing the salvation of Israel; that his death is not in vain. Jesus' reply is full of love and respect: Look at what is happening and at the part you have played in it, he says, and have no doubt that it is really true. The political order did not disappear magically, to be replaced by another one. Earth did not turn into heaven. But the prophetic vision of John the Baptist saw the signs of the kingdom and preached them faithfully; John lived to see the One who fulfilled those signs.

When it comes time to evaluate our lives, isn't ours the same question: have our years on earth meant something? Jesus answers yes, look at what is happening and at the part you played. "No one has arisen greater than John the Baptist; yet the least in the kingdom of heaven is greater than he." Yes, our lives mean something because through Christ we lived in and opened doors to the kingdom.—1989

DECEMBER 18

Luke 3:8. *Do not begin to say to yourselves, "We have Abraham as our ancestor."*

John the Baptist emphasized the personal responsibility of everyone before God. For anyone to claim salvation by virtue of belonging to the chosen people or the chosen church is just not enough. We can claim salvation, yes, but only if we make the effort to respond to the grace that is freely given us. The mere fact of membership in the church is not enough. Indeed, it invites perhaps a more severe judgment than if one had never heard of the church (2 Peter 2:21).

To be a member of Christ in the real sense of the word, to have put on Christ as a garment, to follow in his way, to enter a state of Christian living in which acts of compassion, forgiveness, generosity, and love emerge as naturally and habitually as leaves from a tree—this is what it means to be a Christian, and therefore a member of the church. Grace is free, but living a life of grace day by day is not easy. It calls for self-control and perseverance, and many new beginnings. It is a life of constant turning to Christ and resting in his love, even when there are no outward signs of rest or of much love.—1978

DECEMBER 19

Matthew 1:23. *"They shall name him Emmanuel," which means, "God is with us."*

Here we come face to face with the mystery of the Incarnation: the eternal Deity becoming a member of the human race, by birth from Mary. This does not mean that a human child became fused with divinity or that God was infused into a particular person at a particular time. There can be no change in the species or the identity of an individual. It is as unthinkable for a mere human being to become God as it would be for an animal to become human.

Rather, the eternal God dared to become human at a particular time. That is why he can suffer with us, sacrifice for us, intercede on our behalf. Because he is one of us, he can be our representative. Because he is one with God, he can bring new life for us all. It is a mystery—a stupendous one. It is the great Christian paradox: God stooping low to us so that we might be raised high to God.—1951

DECEMBER 20

Mark 3:5. *Stretch out your hand.*

This phrase appears thirty-two times in the NRSV translation of the Bible. I think anytime something is repeated more than three times, it's probably worth paying extra attention to. In today's story, just as in the other thirty-odd times this phrase is used in the Bible, God is asking us to take an active and physical role in the story of redemption.

When God asks Moses to stretch his hand over the Red Sea to divide it, the children of Israel walk across dry land, freed from the bondage of Egypt. When Jesus asks the man with the withered hand to stretch out his hand, Jesus divides the seas of hard-heartedness.

Jesus shows us that hardness of heart is more crippling and limiting than a withered hand.

The healing Jesus brings refuses to obey anyone's timing, other than his own. Doing the right thing, the right way, for the right reason, with a lack of regard for the date on the calendar or the scorn of others, is one of the chief reasons we love Jesus, and one of the reasons for which he was killed. We should remember that.—2015

DECEMBER 21

John 20:25. *Unless I see the mark of the nails in his hands, and put my finger in the mark of the nails and my hand in his side, I will not believe.*

At this time of year it is easier for people in our secular culture to suspend disbelief. The hardest agnostic soul is softened by Christmas, if only in passing, and faithful people are drawn deep into the heart of their believing as they rejoice in Emmanuel, God with us. Then just before the joy of Christmas we are reminded of Thomas.

Today is the feast of that doubter. Just like a modern pragmatist, Thomas wants evidence. Thomas's presence reminds us that doubt is not God's enemy, that we are free to doubt, that God invites our doubt, that doubting is not the opposite of believing but of a piece with it. The opposite of faith is not doubt but fear. Thomas is not fearful. And Jesus receives him as he is, belief and disbelief mixed in him in just the way it is in most of us. God does not ask us to swallow our doubts. God asks only that we come to Christ day in and day out, unafraid to confess our misgivings, accepted as we are, until we can finally say with Thomas, "My Lord and my God!"—1995

DECEMBER 22

Luke 1:38. *Then Mary said, "Here am I, the servant of the Lord; let it be with me according to your word."*

Mary answered God's call to become a servant of the Lord with hardly any hesitation. What an example she sets for us! How far would I go and how much would I do and what exactly would I give up if faced with such an announcement? If the survival of a friend meant that we had to abandon all of our Christmas plans to drive five hundred miles, would we do it? If the homeless shelter asked for volunteers to spend Christmas Eve, all night, at the shelter, would we volunteer?

God asks much of us. Are we willing to be Christ bearers in our own lives? Are we willing to be what someone described as "Little Christs" as we move through the events of our daily life, as we live in community with all sorts and conditions of people? We, too, can give birth to the light that never goes out, the light of life, the light of love, the light of God in Christ—in us!—1998

DECEMBER 23

Luke 1:41. *When Elizabeth heard Mary's greeting, the child leaped in her womb. And Elizabeth was filled with the Holy Spirit.*

"For while gentle silence enveloped all things, and night in its swift course was now half gone, your all-powerful word leaped from heaven, from the royal throne" (Wisdom of Solomon 18:14-15).

There is a contrast between the thought of God leaping into the world and the calm stillness of that holy night. But there is also something thrilling about God being so concerned with the world, so anxious to save it, not wanting to wait any longer. With joy and anticipation and purpose, God "leaped" down from heaven to become a part of us.

In a way, the word leap is a religious word. Like every woman who ever bore a child, Elizabeth thrilled with new life when the child leaped in her womb. Isn't this our natural response to the beauty of creation? When the Holy Spirit touches us, our whole being leaps with joy and delight. We leap into the world to tell anew the story of a night when all things were in awed silence and the Almighty Word did indeed leap down from heaven.—1976

❧❧❧

DECEMBER 24

Psalm 51:9. *Make me hear of joy and gladness, that the body you have broken may rejoice.*

Mexico and other countries throughout the Spanish-speaking world celebrate Posadas, a beautiful tradition that reenacts Mary and Joseph's search for a place for Jesus to be born. Two children or young people, perhaps dressed in costumes, represent Joseph and Mary. They go from house to house, followed by a crowd of musicians and pilgrims knocking on doors and singing the Posadas song, begging to be given room at the inn.

From inside each house, "innkeepers" reject them, worried the pilgrims may be robbers, until Mary, Joseph, and the pilgrims reach a home where the Holy Family is recognized. The door opens, and a warm welcome with delicious food and drink await them inside.

Posadas is celebrated all over the United States, with many churches embracing this beautiful tradition. Posadas teaches us a beautiful song—a message of joy and gladness: When we receive the weary and the outcast in our homes, we are, oftentimes unknowingly, receiving Jesus too.—2016

DECEMBER 25

Luke 2:15-16. *The shepherds said to one another, "Let us go now to Bethlehem and see this thing that has taken place, which the Lord has made known to us." So they went with haste and found Mary and Joseph, and the child lying in the manger.*

Some of us may be joyfully unwrapping presents in a heap of colored paper or eating and drinking with family or friends. Others may be alone, far separated in space or time from those we love. Whatever may be the case for us, the business of our hearts today should be to find "Mary and Joseph and the child lying in the manger." Where will that manger be for you? Your church, the company of laughing children and loved ones, or the silence of a hospital room or a lonely apartment? Wherever you may be, be sure he is ready to enter your heart. Pray with gratitude and adoration.—1992

DECEMBER 26

Isaiah 61:10. *I will greatly rejoice in the LORD, my whole being shall exult in my God.*

References to joy and exultation abound during the Christmas season. It is not surprising that we should find ways to rejoice when the spirit of Christ is in our midst. But will we continue to spread the joy of the gospel even after this season has passed?

We rejoice specifically that Jesus was born not to be a great teacher, or a faith healer, or a prophet (though he clearly was all of these). And we rejoice that Jesus was born not to be a miracle worker, or a reformer, or an organizer (though he was all of these too). We rejoice that Jesus was born to dwell among us and show us what separates us from God, what splits us apart from one another, and what divides us from ourselves.

Jesus lived, taught, healed, challenged, and proclaimed the love of God in such a way that it turned the world upside down. That is our challenge as well. This Christmas season, indeed at all times, we are commissioned by our faith to "go forth into the world rejoicing in the power of the Spirit." Thanks be to God!—2003

DECEMBER 27

Matthew 23:37. *Jerusalem, Jerusalem, the city that kills the prophets and stones those who are sent to it!*

Jesus' prophetic words about Jerusalem anticipate the stoning of Stephen, the first Christian martyr. Stephen's stoning is also linked to Saul (Paul), who witnesses the event that undoubtedly influenced his own later conversion to become the great apostle to the Gentiles.

An English ballad from the mid-fifteenth century depicts an imaginary conversation between King Herod and Stephen, who, according to the legend, is in the king's employ. Stephen tells Herod he wants to leave to worship the Bethlehem child who "shall help us in our need." Herod replies that is as likely as the chicken on his dinner platter beginning to speak, whereupon the chicken crowed "Christus natus est!" (Christ is born). Herod in his fury orders Stephen stoned.

The story is offered as an explanation for the proximity of the feast of Stephen to Christmas. Stephen was the first in the long line of Christian martyrs including Thomas of Canterbury. Modern martyrs such as Dietrich Bonhoeffer and Archbishop Janani Luwum are memorialized at Canterbury in a simple notebook behind the high altar.—2004

DECEMBER 28

Exodus 33:19. *I will make all my goodness pass before you, and will proclaim before you the name, "The Lord."*

The author of Exodus prefaces this speech by explaining "the Lord used to speak to Moses face to face, as one speaks to a friend." Our lectionary sets John the Baptist's close relationship with Jesus in the context of Moses' relationship to God. In the wilderness, when Moses is weary of the weight of leadership, God refreshes him with an intimate vision of God's very self. Moses, not famous for his unquestioning obedience, needs the reminder of God's goodness. John inherits this pattern of relationship with the Lord. John brings all that he is, his whole person, to Jesus, and Jesus receives him. If the other disciples were disturbed by John's "thunderous" personality, by his questions of Jesus, Jesus himself seems to have known what John needed. Clearly Jesus made his own goodness pass before John. Like Moses and John, we are meant to bring all that we are to God and to talk face to face. Nothing less will satisfy.—1996

DECEMBER 29

Matthew 2:16. *When Herod saw that he had been tricked by the wise men, he was infuriated, and he sent and killed all the children in and around Bethlehem who were two years old or under.*

The horrible crimes against humanity committed by tyrants send chills down our spines. We like to think that the world has made some progress in the past two thousand years, and perhaps it has. Yet the mass murders under totalitarian regimes, which have not— never have—spared children, have reached incredible proportions in our own day. To our shame, nations like our own are also guilty of massacres.

The account of the Holy Innocents is indeed most oddly placed in the calendar. It seems it should come after Epiphany. Yet this is the kind of world into which Jesus was born, and in which his gospel continues to call out for justice, peace, and the end of oppression. "Our help is in the Name of the LORD, the maker of heaven and earth" (Psalm 124:8).—2002

❧❧❧

DECEMBER 30

John 8:7. *Let anyone among you who is without sin be the first to throw a stone at her.*

"What is original sin?" the twelve-year-old asked her grandfather. And he replied, "It is something we all have in common. It is one of the things that holds us together."

Grandfather's definition of original sin was a way of saying what Jesus had in mind when he said, "Let anyone among you who is without sin be the first to throw a stone at her." There is no doubt about the sinfulness of what the woman had done. Jesus understood the destructive consequences of adultery just as much as the scribes and Pharisees. The difference was that when Jesus zeroed in on sin, it was not just the obvious sins that caught his attention. Less obvious, but just as sinful, was the self-righteous finger-pointing of those who sought to condemn the woman.

Hard-heartedness is also a sin, because in its rush to condemn it does not hear the message of mercy and forgiveness from the Savior. Jesus' parting words to the woman—"Neither do I condemn you"— are a reminder of just how forgiving is the God whom we meet in the Bible.—1996

DECEMBER 31

John 8:12. *Again Jesus spoke to them, saying "I am the light of the world. Whoever follows me will never walk in darkness but will have the light of life."*

Light is one of those universal images which, in one way or another, recurs in many religions. Thus, it was no surprise when, in the fourth century, the church selected the Roman celebration of Sol Invictus (December 25) to be the yearly festival of the coming of the True Light into the world. Small children, being tucked into bed, often ask to have the door left open just a crack. "The light shines in the darkness and the darkness did not overcome it" (John 1:5).

Children may not know the words, but intuitively, early in life, we sense light's importance. The light of Jesus is inward, a light known to those who have consciously and deliberately made Jesus their companion. He offers us his presence, his light, in all sorts of places and circumstances, and never more so than when, in the name of Christ, we are called to enter the darkness.—1996

About the Cover Artist

"EDEN," the mosaic on the cover, was created by Kathy Thaden. Her study of fine arts and degree in commercial art led her to a career in broadcast design. For twenty-five years, Kathy worked as television art director, animator, and graphic designer—winning numerous honors for design, including seven Emmy awards.

Seeking something more tactile, Kathy's creativity now comes through her mosaic art. She lives and works in Colorado where her husband is an Episcopal priest. Kathy weaves her passion for modern mosaics together with reflections on God's gift of creativity during her popular Mosaics as Meditation retreats and workshops.

"Working with broken stone or glass is transforming as pieces are changed, made whole again. Finding beauty in brokenness, I treasure discards from our 'throw-away' consumer culture. It's important that nothing be wasted," says Thaden.

A full-time studio artist, Kathy's mosaics range from abstract sculpture and landscapes to liturgical wall hangings and commissioned works. She is a professional member of the Society of American Mosaic Artists, Episcopal Church & Visual Arts, and founding member and past president of Colorado Mosaic Artists. www.thadenmosaics.com

About Forward Movement

Forward Movement is committed to inspiring disciples and empowering evangelists. While we produce great resources like this book, Forward Movement is not a publishing company. We are a ministry. Our mission is to inspire disciples and empower evangelists. Publishing books, daily reflections, studies for small groups, and online resources is an important way that we live out this ministry. More than a half million people read our daily devotions through *Forward Day by Day*, which is also available in Spanish (*Adelante Día a Día*) and Braille, online, as a podcast, and as an app for your smartphones or tablets. It is mailed to more than fifty countries, and we donate nearly 30,000 copies each quarter to prisons, hospitals, and nursing homes. We actively seek partners across the Church and look for ways to provide resources that inspire and challenge. A ministry of The Episcopal Church for eighty years, Forward Movement is a nonprofit organization funded by sales of resources and gifts from generous donors.

To learn more about Forward Movement and our resources, visit us at www.ForwardMovement.org (or www.VenAdelante.org). We are delighted to be doing this work and invite your prayers and support.